# Discover the World of Canine Cognition

## Revolutionize Your Dog's Training and Provide Access to the Brain Candy All Dogs Crave!

Pat Miller, CBCC-KA, CPDT-KA

Wenatchee, Washington U.S.A.

**Discover the World of Canine Cognition**
Revolutionize Your Dog's Training and Provide Access to the Brain Candy All Dogs Crave!
Pat Miller, CBCC-KA, CPDT-KA

Dogwise Publishing
A Division of Direct Book Service, Inc.
403 South Mission Street, Wenatchee, Washington 98801
1-509-663-9115, 1-800-776-2665
www.dogwisepublishing.com / info@dogwisepublishing.com


Interior: Lindsay Davisson
Cover design: Erika Austin





ISBN 9781617812996 Printed in the U.S.A.

# Dedication

This book is dedicated to all those in the world of behavior science and ethology whose studies have furthered our understanding and acceptance of the cognitive abilities of all animals—including but by no means limited to Dr. Charles Henry Turner, Dr. John Pilley, Dame Jane Morris Goodall, Dr. Adam Miklosi, Dr. Claudia Fugazza, Dr. Alexandra Horowitz, Dr. Brian Hare, and more. Also, to all the animal training and behavior professionals who are embracing animal cognition and incorporating it into their work to further enhance the quality of life for the animals who share our world.

# Table of Contents

# More Praise for

# *Discover the World of Canine Cognition*

---

*Discover the World of Canine Cognition* is this fascinating, cutting-edge exploration into the mysterious world "inside a dog's mind." In compelling accounts of dogs reading, counting, matching, and imitating us, this landmark book bridges the gap between what scientists and dog lovers alike have long suspected and what we now know—dogs are very, very smart indeed. Practical enrichment games with step-by-step instructions woven in with knowledge about dog learning and agency in husbandry make this book a "must have" for both your "brain candy" and research dog libraries. The critical topics for understanding and helping our dogs, such as learning body language, incorporating scent searches, and consent testing are brilliantly illustrated in this gift to dogs and the people who love them. Anyone, pet parent or trainer, who likes to stay up to speed on both the fun and the science of dog training has this golden opportunity to learn from one of the most influential leading voices in dog welfare and training, Pat Miller. Highly recommended.

**Linda Michaels,** M.A., Experimental Psychology, author of *The Do No Harm Dog Training and Behavior Handbook*

Your dog is smarter than you think, so prepare to be amazed as you experiment at home with Pat Miller's terrific new guide to canine cognition. The fun reason to dive into this engaging new book is that it'll teach you how to show off with your dog! But the beautiful reason to start teaching what Miller calls "brain candy games" is that it will open an entirely new world to you both—one that offers enrichment, engagement, and plain old joy all right in your own home. What if, the next time your friends are over, you casually asked your dog to go get the yellow frisbee in the bedroom—and he did it? What if you followed that by asking him to go find your keys—and he did? And then grabbed the stack of cards on the table, showed your dog the one that said "SPIN"—and he spun? Get Pat Miller's beginner-friendly introduction to canine cognition and within weeks, you and your suddenly no-longer-bored dog could be showing off as a team, and feeling closer than ever. As a dog trainer, I can immediately think of so many clients for whom Pat Miller's terrific new book on canine cognition could be a lifeline:

- The one whose young dog is acting out because he's bored
- The one who could use a jump-start with training, because "sit-down-stay" feels stale
- The one whose dog is recovering from surgery and their usual physical adventures are on hold
- The retired couple who are a bit more home-bound than they anticipated, but still want to provide top-notch engagement for their dog
- The folks whose reactive dog is taking time to adjust to city life and who need great ideas for building their relationship at home

Miller shows readers how to teach dogs cute games like how to pick their topping (chicken or peanut butter) with a nose indication, but one of my favorite things about this book is that she doesn't stop there. She helps readers follow that thought along, encouraging them to realize there are dozens of times a day where their dog could be making a choice—right path or left path? Bowser or Fluffy? town or marina?—and that they can use their new skills to give their dog more real-life agency. The more we listen to our dogs' choices, the more we find those "behavior problems" seem to fade away!

**Kathy Callahan**, CPDT-KA, LFDM, author of *Welcoming Your Puppy from Planet Dog*

*Discover the World of Canine Cognition* may be an intimidating title when you first pick up this book, especially to newcomers to the dog training world. However, wherever you are on your journey in the dog world, this book makes the topic of canine cognition not only easy to understand, but enjoyable to implement into your life with your dog. If you've picked up this book, you've most likely learned you can teach your dog to be a willing participant in nail trimming and brush, but did you know you can also teach them how to read or how to bring you your green slippers from the living room to the bedroom? This book will help you teach your dog to do just that and more! Or maybe you are a seasoned dog trainer? This book will help you remember there is still joy and fun to be had in the dog training world. We haven't yet discovered all our dogs are capable of. *Discover the World of Canine Cognition* and discover more about the furry friend at your feet.

**Karen Chapdelaine**, IAABC-CDBC/ADT, CPDT-KA, DN-CET, FFCP, owner The Timeless Dog, LLC

This book is a wonderful tool that explains the science, development and history of Canine Cognition, along with giving clear and concise training directions for the many skills and processes for the various cognition activities! A great book for the dog enthusiast as well as trainers wanting to explore this topic a bit more!

**Sonia Fetherling,** CPDT, CAP 1 and CAP 2, LFDM, FFCP, owner of Best Of Behavior, LLC. Dog Training and Behavior Consulting

Like many of Pat Miller's books, *Canine Cognition* is an easy read packed full of mind-blowing nuggets of information. This book highlights the powerful ability of our dogs to think and creatively solve problems. Not only does she discuss the untapped potential of our best friends, she also offers many fun exercises to try with your own dog. I'll admit that I got so caught up in trying out her Brain Candy Games that I almost missed out on offering my endorsement of this book. After doing several exercises with my dogs, I can honestly say this book is an exciting and fun addition to my collection, and I'm looking forward to working my way through all of the exercises.

**Drake L. Azevedo**, CBCC-KA, CPDT-KA

# Acknowledgments

This book has come to fruition thanks in large part to the ongoing encouragement from friends, family, mentors, peers, clients and students who have supported my dive into the world of canine cognition. Far too many to name, you have tested and confirmed the protocols laid out in the pages that follow. You know who you are, and many of you are included in the photos in this book.

And thanks always, and forever to my beloved husband, Paul, who is everything to me in my world, who makes all things possible, and has for the past three-plus decades (with more to come!), plus to the sixteen dogs who have shared our life together during those 39 years, each important for my understanding of canine cognition:

- Mandy—Rough Collie
- Keli—Australian Kelpie
- Dusty—Pomeranian
- Smokie—German Shepherd mix
- Josie—Terrier mix
- Tucker—Cattle Dog mix
- Katie—Australian Kelpie
- Dubhy—Scottish Terrier
- Lucy (Footloose and Fancy Free)—Cardigan Corgi
- Bonnie Wee Lass—Scorgidoodle
- Scooter—Pomeranian

- Missy—Australian Shepherd
- Kaizen—Australian Kelpie
- Sunny (Sunshine Lollipops and Rainbows)—Pomeranian
- Kelpie Chaos (KC)—Australian Kelpie
- Jiffy Pop—Terrier mix

And eternal thanks to Dogwise, for publishing my books!

# Introduction
# How Cognition Came to the World of Dogs

Welcome to the wonderful world of canine cognition! **Cognition** includes all conscious and unconscious processes such as problem solving, memorizing and reasoning. The recognition that dogs have these abilities is a relatively new—and very exciting—development in the field of dog training and behavior. Twenty years ago you wouldn't have heard the words "canine" and "cognition" in the same sentence! Today there are canine cognition labs all over the world, and we know that our canine family members (as well as other species) are capable of amazing feats of cognition. Eagerly jumping on this bandwagon, we in the training and behavior profession are incorporating cognition into our training and behavior modification programs—and having a ton of fun while doing so.

## The way it used to be

How I wish we knew then what we know now. I think many of you will identify with my story. I have worked professionally with animals for more than 50 years, starting in the horse world riding hunters and jumpers, then twenty years working at the Marin Humane Society in Novato, California. I was a Humane Officer/Animal Control Officer for a good part of that time—I got to rescue animals and arrest people who were mean to animals! Finally, I have worked for more than 25 years as an animal training and behavior professional with my own business, Peaceable Paws (and still going strong).

*My first career—hunters and jumpers!*

*My second career—rescuing animals, arresting people who were mean to animals, teaching humane education in schools.*

*Saving baby Sarah Jo from the livestock auction.*

I am what we call a "crossover trainer." Decades ago, I trained using what I now call old-fashioned methods—choke chains, collar corrections, even the horrible "alpha roll." (No, I never used shock or prongs on my dogs …) I was good at it. My dogs and I earned numerous titles in obedience competition with scores in the upper 190s (out of a possible 200 points). I loved my dogs, and I believe they loved me—even though I now know that they also feared me, at least to some degree. In my defense, in those days that's how *everyone* trained.

I crossed over to **force-free training**—that eschews the use of aversive tools and compulsion—after my beloved Terrier mix Josie *(Do You Know the Way to San Jose* CD, CDX) hid under our back deck rather than submit to one more ear pinch—the old-fashioned pain-causing technique I was using to try to force her to fetch the metal dumbbell that she hated. She was required to retrieve a metal dumbbell for the scent discrimination exercise she needed to learn to earn her Utility Degree (UD) that we were aiming for. I quit training that day, started learning about positive reinforcement/force-free training, and have never looked back.

*Josie, my force-free mentor.*

Thanks to the pioneers in the development of effective, force-free dog training techniques: Karen Pryor, Jean Donaldson and many more, there are now thousands of trainers (including me) who use, teach, preach and promote force-free training. In the past few decades, the modern dog-loving community has learned a lot about the value of creating relationships with dogs based on voluntary cooperation, built on a foundation of mutual trust and respect and are happily sharing that with other dog-lovers. And horse-lovers. And cat-lovers. And more.

We learned about the "four quadrants of operant-conditioning" and realized that the tools many of us had successfully used in the past, such as choke chains and prong collars, and verbal and physical punishment, worked because they suppressed behavior through positive punishment. They taught the dog that if he did the wrong thing we would hurt or intimidate him. See Chapter 5 for a more detailed discussion of operant-conditioning.

We learned to ask questions. Not just, "Does this work?" but "Why does this work?" and the very important "Is this something I am willing to do to my dog?"

We learned that there was an entire body of science behind dog training and behavior. We eagerly embraced science and learned about behavior analysis, unconditioned responses, classical conditioning, operant-conditioning and much more. We started seeking credentials to distinguish ourselves from the less-educated old-fashioned trainers.

## The intersection of behavior and learning

Modern training is based on an understanding of this fascinating science of behavior and learning. This has kept me invigorated about working in this profession; it never gets old or boring because science is always discovering new things about behavior and ways we can apply them in our work with our amazing canine family members. In recent years, just as training was perhaps beginning to feel a little stale … along came canine cognition!

Our dogs' cognitive abilities were first brought to the attention of the general public in 2011 by a Border Collie named Chaser. Chaser had the incredibly good fortune to be adopted by Dr. John Pilley, a retired psychologist who decided to use his now bountiful free time to train his dog and dabble in canine cognition. In fact, he did much more than dabble—he opened the world's eyes to the cognitive potential of our dogs and a whole new way of working with, understanding and relating to our canine companions, not to mention writing a great book.

Chaser is widely known as the dog who amassed the largest canine vocabulary ever—an impressive 1022 proper nouns—primarily the names of her very large collection of toys. This process of learning new words and concepts with minimal exposure to new information is known as fast-mapping, and prior to Chaser, dogs weren't given much credit for **fast-mapping** abilities. Chaser opened our eyes. Not only was she able to learn the names of new toys with lightning speed, but she was also able to understand full sentences and use deductive reasoning. When presented with a pile of toys that she knew, plus one that was new to her, she was able to pick out the new one when it was named, simply by process of elimination. She knew the names of all the others so the "thingamajig" must be this one!

"Of course," you might say, "she was brilliant because she was a Border Collie and she belonged to a psychologist!" But no … now some fifteen years after Chaser first hit the world stage, plenty of "ordinary dogs" who live with regular humans are accomplishing all kinds of extraordinary cognitive feats, including reading, writing, counting, imitation, and much more.

I have been training dogs since looooong before Chaser opened our eyes to the potential of the canine brain. I now teach cognition classes, cognition workshops and cognition academies. I love it. The dogs love it. Their humans love it. What's not to love? You and your dog will love it too. So, no more delay! Let's jump into the pages of this book, explore the incredible potential of your dog's brain, find out what you and your dog have been missing, gain a much deeper understanding of how your dog's mind works and get ready to share in the joy of canine cognition!

# Part 1
## What is Cognition?

# Chapter 1
# The History of Canine Cognition Research

Do you know that you can teach your dog to read? To count? To imitate you? Welcome to the wonderful world of canine cognition where our dogs do this and much more! We used to think our dogs were not capable of complex thoughts and emotions. We've come a long way in our understanding and appreciation of our dogs' brains and how we can work with them in our training and behavior modification programs.

It's been quite a climb, and cognition is just the latest rung on the ladder; I predict we still have even more exciting discoveries in the future. The better we understand our dogs, the better our lives and relationships with them can be. We have, indeed, come a long way from old-fashioned force-based training to cooperative methods that give our dogs choice and **agency** (the ability to exercise individual control and autonomy in decision-making and actions) and a much better quality of life … and we still have a long way to go.

Here are the types of research that have been conducted to measure various aspects of a dog's cognitive abilities.

## Can a dog feel pain?

Do you think your dog can feel pain? Your cat? Your horse? Well of course they can, everybody knows that!!!

Yet there was a time when scientists and philosophers told us that animals don't feel pain. Seventeenth century philosopher Renee Descartes in 1637 argued that animals deserve no direct concern because animals are not conscious, therefore they have no interests or well-being to take into account when considering the effects of our actions. He stated that any behaviors that might appear to be pain responses were simply automatic body responses that didn't involve pain. Indeed, he held that animals were "automata" rather than feeling beings. Due in large part to this widely accepted (and totally unscientific, unsupported) theory, unthinkable acts of cruelty were inflicted on companion animals, livestock and wildlife over centuries to the detriment of our relationships with them.

During the eighteenth century that idea began to very slowly change. Philosophers started to accept the notion that animals could feel pain. By the end of the nineteenth century, scientists and philosophers had developed a more sophisticated concept of sentience, which opened the door to scientific consideration that animals might feel pain.

However, even into the 1970s, some scientists claimed that it was sentimentalism to believe animals could experience suffering, and many veterinary schools were still teaching their students that animals feel pain "differently" than humans do. Fortunately, over the last fifty years it has become more widely accepted that many animal species do, in fact, experience pain on a par with our human pain experience. While there are still far too many troglodyte holdouts who dispute these facts, science today is telling us that even some of the last holdout species (including fish and insects) do feel pain. Some studies have even demonstrated that plants react to stimuli in a possibly pain-related way, although they have stopped short of claiming that plants can feel pain.

One must wonder how animals could have ever survived if they didn't feel pain? Our modern-day acceptance of animal pain underlies the emphasis on prevention and relief of pain in guidelines and laws on humane care and supports the focus on better treatment of animals in general, including, but not limited to, our beloved canine companions and the training methods we use with them.

## Can a dog use tools?

"Well then," we were told somewhat grudgingly in the 1970s, "perhaps animals can feel pain, but only humans make and use tools …" Wrong! The amazing work of Dr. Jane Goodall and many other modern **ethologists** (scientists who study the behavior of animals in their natural environment) has proven that not only can non-human primates make and use tools, but so can a wide variety of other animal species. There are a number of online videos of Caledonian Crows making and using tools. One of my favorites (I show it to my academy classes) is of a Caledonian Crow in a laboratory taking a straight piece of wire and trying to use it to pull a basket out of a long plastic tube. The basket has food in it that the crow would like to eat, but of course a straight wire won't hook the basket handle. The crow pulls out the wire, looks at it, takes it over to the side of the table and bends it into a hook; voila, she just made a tool! She then uses it to reach down into the tube, pull out the basket and proceeds to eat the food. If you go to YouTube and enter "Crow" and "Tools" in the search box, you can find this and many others of crows using tools. And if you enter "Animals" and "Tools" you can find dozens of video examples of all sorts of other species making and using tools as well.

Another favorite tool maker/user is the octopus, who has also demonstrated the ability to make and use tools to get food in laboratory studies. Even insects use tools! Ants using tools was first documented in 1976. Researchers observed ants using absorbent objects like soil, leaves and small twigs to absorb liquid food so they can carry it back to their nests. Therapy dogs turn lights on and off and manipulate other tools for their human charges. One of my favorite Facebook videos is from a shelter camera that captured footage of a dog opening her own kennel and then going around the shelter and letting all the other dogs out. And how about your own favorite canine companion? There's a great video of a Border Collie and a Belgian Malinois using plates to play a game with a ball. Guess what? If your dog has learned to jump up on your door to push down on the latch and escape the house, rides a skateboard, or pulls a wagon with a rope she holds in her mouth … she is *using* tools!

## Does a dog have emotions?

"Okay," scientists used to tell us, "all this is incredibly fascinating and amazing, but surely animals don't have emotions that impact their behaviors!" In the past, you would be accused of being **anthropomorphic**—a very dirty word in scientific circles—if you tried to attribute human-like emotions to animals. They don't possibly have the same emotional responses we do. Or … do they …? Well, apparently our dogs—and other animals—do share much the same range of emotions that we humans do. In fact, it's damn arrogant of our species to claim emotions for ourselves—they aren't human emotions, they are just *emotions*. And yes, animals do have them.

*Dogs do have emotions.*

Current research has demonstrated that many species, including our beloved canines, share brain circuitry very similar to the human parts of the brain that control emotion—the **amygdala** and the **periaqueductal grey**. While there's no doubt among most dog lovers that dogs have emotions, this concept is still being discussed in the halls of academia. Some insist that even though animals show emotional behaviors that we can observe, we can't assume the behaviors mean the animals who display them have emotional feelings. (I don't know how anyone can think of this, but apparently some scientists really do!) Others, such as the esteemed neurobiologist Dr. Jaak Panskepp of Washington State University (the guy who tickled rats to demonstrate animal emotion), argue that if it walks like a duck and quacks like a duck—it probably is a duck!

Just ask anyone who shares their home and their heart with dogs: "Can your dog be happy? Sad? Scared?" Any animal lover will tell you that of course they can. And guess what? Those are emotions. And yes, the scientific community is coming to accept this as well, although there is still considerable debate in that community on the topic. While the jury is still out as to whether dogs and other animals can love the *same* way humans do, I'm willing to bet there will be a time in the not-too-distant future that we agree that they can and do. Two books recently published on this subject that are worth reading are *Mood Matters* by Karin Pienaar and *How Dogs Love Us* by Gregory Burns. They can be ordered on Dogwise.com.

## Are dogs cognitive?

So … what about cognition? Cognition has been the last holdout in our understanding and acceptance of other animals as **sentient**; thinking, feeling organisms worthy of far more respect and consideration than we have given them in the past. Now science tells us that many species are, indeed, cognitive—capable of a variety of complex thought processes. Insects, for example, have long been thought to display only the simplest forms of learning, but recent experimental studies, especially in social insects, have suggested that they are capable of various forms of sophisticated cognition. Even as far back as the early 1900s some forward-thinking scientists were proposing that insects were cognitive. American zoologist and comparative psychologist Charles Henry Turner, who died in 1923, was one of the first scientists to attribute cognition to animals considered unlikely to possess it. His primary study subjects were arthropods such as spiders and bees and his research was focused on engaging them in pioneering experiments that suggested cognitive abilities were more complex than most scientists of that era believed were possible for non-human species. Turner also explored differences in the behavior of individuals within those species, a quality today referred to as **personality**.

Once again, common sense would tell us that to survive, all species need to be able to perform the various functions associated with cognition—problem solving, grasping and applying concepts and more.

We know now that our dogs can reason, they can problem-solve, they can grasp concepts and much more. Read on to learn more about canine cognition, the fascinating capabilities of our dogs' brains, the ways we can work with their cognitive powers and how you can incorporate cognition into your relationship with your dog.

# Chapter 2

# The Animal Mind

## I Know You Know, We Know They Know

---

### One more cognitive door opens

The question of "mind," or **metacognition**, has also been under significant scrutiny in the dog world as our acceptance and appreciation of the canine brain has advanced. "Mind" has three fundamental properties:

- **Self-awareness**—Experiences "self" in the real world.
- **Volition**—Deliberate behavior; intentionality, seeking, desire, interest, and expectancy.
- **Consciousness**—The capacity for self-consciousness, includes questions about "theory of mind" in non-human animals and whether animals are capable of attributing mental states to others.

Hard scientific evidence of canine meta-cognition has been harder to come by than canine emotion. The same brain circuits that exist in humans are present in many other animals, suggesting that "mind" likely exists for them as well. Our friend Dr. Jakk Panskepp argued that animals do possess at least some degree of metacognition, and that the answer to this question will become clearer with continued neurobiological and cognitive study. Indeed, some aspects of the canine mind seem inarguable. Does anyone doubt that dogs have volition? If it walks like a duck …

In fact, advances in the study of animal cognition over the past decade-plus are confirming for us that the minds of dogs and other non-human animals *do* possess the fundamental properties of self-awareness, volition and consciousness. These are all concepts that will come into play as we introduce you to Brain Candy Games in the coming chapters. Hold onto your leash—you're in for some eye-opening surprises!

## Self-awareness

Scientists have long used the "mirror test" as proof of self-awareness—the physical demonstration of the mind experiencing self in the real world. Put a dot of paint on a toddler's face and show him a mirror—the toddler will touch the dot on his *own* face; he realizes that it is *himself* upon whose face he sees the dot in the mirror. Animals that pass the mirror test will typically adjust their positions so that they can get a better look at the new mark on their body and may even touch it or try to remove it. They usually pay much more attention to the part of their body that bears a new marking.

Other primates—Bonobos, Chimpanzees, Orangutans and Gorillas, were the first non-human animals to be observed passing the mirror test. Since those early days, several other species have also passed, including the Asian Elephant, Bottlenose Dolphins, Orca Whales, Eurasian Magpies, Cleaner Fish and … wait for it … ants. Yes, ants.

Certainly, dogs must be able to do this, right? Yes, but only if we accept that there are other ways to demonstrate self-awareness. Since dogs are much more aware of their world through their sense of smell than their vision, the mirror test doesn't really apply to them. Instead, their sense of self-awareness appears to be derived through scent rather than sight.

Professor Alexandra Horowitz is a canine cognition researcher who heads the Dog Cognition Lab at Barnard College. She is well known for her excellent books on understanding the world of dogs and has conducted research on dogs' self-awareness through smell. Horowitz's work suggests that dogs do, indeed, have a level of self-awareness that can be demonstrated through their sense of smell. Horowitz says, "Dogs are olfactory creatures, not visual; they need a smell mirror. So that's the kind of thing I tried to design." She has determined in her works that dogs investigate their own odors longer when modified in an 'olfactory mirror test' and concluded that, "Such behavior implies a recognition of the odor as being of or from themselves." Horowitz has written several books on why dogs do what they do. Her book *Inside of a Dog* (available at Dogwise.com) is full of this type of research and is presented in readable fashion.

Regardless of the mode of measuring self-awareness, I think we're now on safe ground to say that we are pretty sure dogs have it.

## Volition

Several qualities that describe volition in dogs include:

- **Intentionality**
- **Seeking**
- **Desire**
- **Interest**
- **Expectancy**

The naysayers of more than a decade ago argued that dogs weren't capable of volition because volition requires a rational mind (the ability to make deliberate decisions) it requires 'reason.' Welcome to the new world of canine cognition where we now accept that dogs can reason, they can act with intention and interest, they are capable of seeking outcomes and they can have desires and expectations. As with so many other cognitive abilities we once declined to grant to dogs and other animals, most dog-lovers would have said "Duh!"—even decades ago.

Volition means that a dog can and will make choices when given the opportunity to do so. In the past, many dog trainers and caretakers kept rigid control over their dog's environment and behaviors—dogs were not permitted to make choices often, if at all. Most trainers are implementing choice in many of our training and behavior protocols with our dogs these days. Read the next chapter to find out more about how we can develop a dog's volitional skills through encouraging choice and agency in their lives.

## Consciousness

Consciousness relates to your dog's ability to be aware of his own thoughts, i.e., self-consciousness is the ability to attribute mental states to others, known as theory of mind. There is no longer any doubt that dogs have an awareness of their own thoughts. We are still exploring how deeply dogs can dive into theory of mind. **Theory of mind** has different levels:

- **I know.** This refers to your dog's awareness of his own thoughts.
- **I know *you* know**. This refers to your dog's awareness of your thoughts. We believe dogs are at least capable of this level of theory of mind. Your dog looks at you and is thinking, "I know you know it's dinner time." "I know you know the Frisbee is up on that bookshelf."
- **I know *you* know *I* know.** This level is a "maybe" for dogs. As in, "I know *you* know I want to go outside." "I know *you* know I hid the ball under the sofa."—and it continues from there with increasingly complex levels.

I'm not aware that we have evidence that dogs are capable of more complex levels of theory of mind than this—but I wouldn't rule it out! We keep discovering that we've been selling our dogs' brains short, and it wouldn't surprise me to find out this is no exception. So, what does your dog know? What does your dog know you know? What do you know your dog knows? Hmmmm. …

# Chapter 3

# Cognition, Agency, and Consent

## When No Means No

---

**Cognition** (from the Latin *cognitio*, meaning knowledge, perception, trial) is defined as mental processes that include knowing, thinking, learning, memory, knowledge formation, reasoning, problem-solving, judging, decision-making, comprehension, grasping and applying concepts, theory of mind and production of language through thought and the senses. That's a lot of brain work! Obviously, we have known for a long time that our dogs are capable of learning and remembering—otherwise any training would have been an impossible task—but the more complex cognitive functions were long considered to be well beyond our dogs' abilities. Not anymore.

A decade ago, you would likely not have heard the words "canine" and "cognition" in the same sentence. Today, as scientific interest in canine cognition has sparked, there are canine cognition laboratories all over the world.

**Canine cognition labs**

- Horowitz Dog Cognition Lab, Barnard College, Columbia University: https://dogcognition.weebly.com/
- The Duke Canine Cognition Center: https://evolutionaryanthropology.duke.edu/research/dogs

- Canine Cognition Center at Yale University: https://doglab.yale.edu/
- Boston College Canine Cognition Center: https://sites.bc.edu/doglab/
- Transylvania University Pioneering Pups Canine Cognition Lab: https://www.transy.edu/dog-lab/
- Brown University Dog Lab: https://sites.brown.edu/browndoglab/
- Arizona Canine Cognition Center: https://dogs.arizona.edu/
- Sacred Heart University Canine Cognition Lab: https://www.sacredheart.edu/academics/colleges--schools/college-of-arts--sciences/departments/psychology/canine-cognition-lab/
- University of Nebraska Canine Cognition and Human Interaction Lab: https://dogcog.unl.edu/
- Dog Cognition Centre, University of Portsmouth, UK: https://www.port.ac.uk/research/research-groups-and-centres/dog-cognition-centre
- Family Dog Project, Eötvös Loránd University, Budapest, Hungary: https://ethology.elte.hu/Family_Dog_Project
- Clever Dog Lab, Messerli Research Institute, Austria: https://www.vetmeduni.ac.at/en/cognition/clever-dog-lab

And many more!

Many of these institutions offer "citizen science" canine cognition programs that you can get involved in with your own dog—some in person and some with online programs. Dr. Brian Hare's Cognition Center at Duke University was among the first to do this with his own "Dognition" program, which is now available online. You can check out the resources listed in the sidebar above to find a cognition lab near you if you want to dive deeper into a scientific exploration of your dog's amazing cognitive powers.

## Agency/choice and control

We now accept dogs (and other species) as sentient creatures and complex thinkers. As we have come to understand that dogs can do far more than just respond to cues such as "sit" "down" and "come," we are also realizing that that we have a greater responsibility to respect their wishes whenever it is possible to do so. This means giving them agency defined as the feeling of control over actions and their consequences. It means, to the extent possible, letting them make their own choices in their lives.

*You choose!*

The wonderful Dr. Susan G. Friedman, Ph.D. is a professor emeritus in the Department of Psychology at Utah State University. (You can find her at: www.behaviorworks.org/ ) She has co-authored chapters on behavior change in five veterinary texts, teaches seminars and courses on animal learning online (How Behavior Works: Living & Learning with Animals) and consults with zoos and animal organizations around the world.

My all-time favorite Dr. Friedman quote is, "The power to control one's own outcomes is essential to behavioral health."

Think about that. Our dogs have very little opportunity for choice in their lives in today's world. We tell them when to eat, when they can play, when and where to urinate and defecate, what to chew on, when and where to sleep. We expect them to walk politely on leash without exploring the rich and fascinating world around them and we want them to lie quietly on the floor for much of the day. Compare this to the lives dogs used to live: running around the farm, chasing squirrels and bunnies at will, eating and rolling in deer, cow and horse poop, chewing on sticks, digging in the mud, swimming in the pond, following the tractor, etc.

There's a good likelihood that this lack of choice is at least partly responsible for the increasing amounts of stress, arousal, reactivity and aggression we are seeing in many of our canine companions these days. Imagine how stressed you would be if your life was as tightly controlled as your dog's! The more choice and agency we can offer them the healthier they will be mentally, and the better our quality of life together.

One simple way to give your dog more choices in his life is to take him for a "Sniffari" instead of a regimented walk. I recall seeing a great cartoon where a dog is marching in perfect heel position down the sidewalk next to his human, looking sad and bored. The thought bubble over the dog's head says, "Whose walk is this, anyway?" What if, instead, you let your dog control the walk as long as he isn't dragging you down the sidewalk? If he wants to stop and sniff … let him! He'll tell you when he's ready to move on. Use a non-retractable long line (a 20-to-50-foot leash that allows him to *really* explore his world) when you're in an appropriate open space. When you walk in the park, let *him* decide which way to go as he follows bunny trails through the grass. You never know what he might find …

I recall one such walk with my Kelpie, Kai. He put his nose to the ground and zig-zagged back and forth for several minutes, clearly following a trail of some kind. After several minutes of tracking, he finally stopped, nose-to-nose with an Eastern Box Turtle.

*The author's Sunny and Kai on Sniffari.*

*Kai finds a turtle.*

Of course, there are times when you need your dog to follow *your* walking agenda. For those occasions I have a different cue. For my dogs, the old stand-by "Heel" still means "I need you to walk right by my left side," while "Let's walk!" means "We're going on a Sniffari!" Some people even use a different leash or collar/harness to let the dog know it's a formal walk versus sniff time. And yes—these are cognitive concepts—that the dog can recognize and understand the meaning of the different cues and pieces of equipment.

Another option for agency for your dog is to simply give him off-leash opportunities where he can run and sniff to his heart's content. If his off-leash recall is reliable and he is dog-friendly, kudos to you! There may be areas of large open dog-friendly acreage in your community where you can take him. If his recall isn't all that great there may be fenced-in dog parks … but beware—unless they are well-run, dog parks can be fraught with hazards for your dog. Sadly there are far too many people who will bring dogs to these parks that aren't suitable for group interactions and walk around texting on their phones rather than paying attention to their dogs. If you need an enclosed area and your own yard is small, or you don't have one, or you just want to give your dog additional adventures, there is a company called **Sniffspot** that contracts with local property owners all over the United States to rent out their spaces to dogs and their humans—yards, acreage, trails, some fenced, some not—at an hourly rate. (Rates vary depending on the host.) You can look for a Sniffspot near you at : https://www.sniffspot.com/

Let's take a deeper dive into how you can give your dog choice and consent, and all the other fascinating aspects of canine cognition. While you read on, start making a life list for your dog of all the different ways you can give him opportunities for choice and agency. Then start putting them into practice.

# Chapter 4
# The Ways Dogs Learn

Before we take a deeper dive into the amazing world of canine cognition, let's take a step back and review a couple of basic but very important concepts about how dogs (and other sentient beings) think and learn. For many years, we in the dog training world have focused on two basic forms of learning—Classical and Operant-conditioning.

## Classical-conditioning

You may remember hearing about the Russian scientist, Ivan Pavlov. He is widely remembered for discovering how a neutral stimulus (like a bell) can become associated with a relevant stimulus (like food) and elicit a conditioned response (like salivation). The response can be emotional (yay, food is coming!) and/or physiological (drooling) and it can trigger a related **Operant** (deliberate) behavior—perhaps the dogs ran to the fronts of their kennels to await the food delivery. Ironically, Pavlov was not a behaviorist—he was studying the digestive system of dogs, specifically the role of saliva in digestion. His lab assistants would bring the food in to cause the dogs to salivate, and Pavlov soon realized that the dogs were salivating before the food even arrived because the emotional part of the brain (the amygdala) had made the association between the bell ringing and the arrival of the food. As a result of this discovery, he articulated the principle of **classical-conditioning**. In clicker training, charging the clicker is classical-conditioning—associating the sound of the click with the delivery of a treat.

Classical-conditioning happens in the real world all the time. As described above, it is simply creating an association between two stimuli. In essence, it is the world operating on the dog; the dog has no real control over the response. In the morning at our house my husband goes out to the barn to start morning chores, and when he's ready for the dogs to come, he messages my phone. When our Australian Kelpie, KC (short for Kelpie Chaos) hears the message beep sound she gets excited and happy and charges to the back door so I can let her out, then beelines full speed to the barn. She has made a very positive classical association between the sound of beeping and the joy of playing in the barn, which triggers running to the door and then the barn.

Positive classical associations are generally a good thing. We want our dogs to be happy about the world around them. One of the best applications of Classical-conditioning is puppy socialization—giving your puppy a positive classical association with the world by taking her lots of places, meeting lots of people, walking on lots of different surfaces, hearing lots of sounds, and making sure she is having a good time while doing all those things. I like to say that a well-socialized dog is an optimist—she believes the world is a happy place, and that anything new she encounters she believes is good and safe unless it proves otherwise. An unsocialized or under socialized dog is a pessimist—she has a negative association with the world, and anything new is bad and scary unless you can convince her otherwise.

*A well-socialized dog is a great companion!*

Negative classical associations are usually not so good. For example, lots of dogs have a very negative association with the sound of thunder, which often generalizes to other signs of pending storms, such as clouds, rain and wind, and possibly changes in barometric pressure. Many dogs experience extreme fear, even panic, at the onset of a storm. Our KC is one—if given the opportunity, when she hears thunder (or fireworks, or gunshots) she will scale over our five-foot tall barn gate and race down our half-mile driveway toward the road. (Obviously we try not to let this happen—she doesn't get to go to the barn when there's a storm brewing.) Fortunately, she also has a very positive association with cars, so when she takes off we leap into our car and head down the driveway after her, and when she sees the car she'll turn around and come running back to leap into the safety of the back seat. Phew!

*Negative classical associations can cause significant behavior challenges.*

## Counter-conditioning

**Counter-conditioning** is a subset of Classical-conditioning in which we work to convince the dog that what he thinks is a bad thing can really be a good thing—i.e., we try to change the negative association to positive. (There are a few situations where we may try to change positive to negative, but it's usually the other way around.) Let's say your dog is not fond of children. You start by managing your dog's world so she doesn't have to interact with children. **Management** is a critically important piece of any behavior modification program because continued exposure to a negative stimulus can sensitize the dog even more. Then you determine your dog's threshold distance—that distance at which she can see a child, be a little concerned, but not have a strong emotional response—she is not barking, lunging or trying to run away, and certainly not trying to bite the child! At that distance, every time she looks at the child you immediately put a small piece of very high value treat right in front of her nose (chicken works well for most dogs). Eventually her brain makes a new association: "That child makes chicken happen!!" Over time, you gradually come closer to the child (this is called "increasing the intensity of stimulus") and then do it with lots of different children, until your dog thinks kids are pretty cool.

*Counter-conditioning this dog's negative association with men.*

Here's a step-by-step description of Counter-conditioning:

1. Determine the distance at which your dog can be in the presence of the child (or other emotion-triggering stimulus) and be alert or wary but not extremely fearful. This is called the threshold distance.
2. While holding your dog on leash, have a helper present the stimulus at this threshold distance. The instant your dog sees the stimulus, feed a bit of chicken, pause, let her look again, feed a bit of chicken, pause, let her look again, feed a bit of chicken, pause, let her look again, non-stop for several seconds
3. Have the helper remove the stimulus and stop feeding chicken.
4. Keep repeating steps 2-3 until the presentation of the stimulus at that distance consistently causes your dog to look at you with a happy smile and a "Yay! Where's my chicken?" expression. This is a conditioned emotional response

(CER)—your dog's association with the stimulus at threshold distance is now positive instead of negative.

5. Now increase the intensity of the stimulus. You can do that by decreasing the distance slightly; by increasing movement of the stimulus at the same distance (a child walking, skipping, or swinging her arms); by increasing the number of stimuli (two or three children, instead of one); increasing the visual "threat" (a tall man instead of a short one, or a man with a beard instead of a clean-shaven one); or by increasing volume (if it's a stimulus that makes noise, such as a vacuum cleaner). I prefer to decrease distance first, in small increments, by moving the dog closer to the location where the stimulus will appear, achieving your CER at each new distance, until your dog is happy to be very near to the non-moving stimulus, perhaps even sniffing or targeting to it.
6. Return to your original threshold distance and again increase the intensity of your stimulus, but with a different element (move the vacuum a little; have two children instead of one; have the man put on a hat or a backpack), gradually decreasing distance and attaining CERs along the way, until your dog is delighted to have the moderately intense stimulus in close proximity.
7. Now, back to your original threshold distance, increase intensity again, by having your helper turn the vacuum on briefly, feed treats the instant it's on, then turn it off and stop the treats. (Or turn up the volume, or add more children, etc.)
8. Repeat until you have the CER, then gradually increase the length of time you have your dog in the presence of the increased-intensity stimulus, until she's happy (but not aroused) to have it present continuously.
9. Begin decreasing distance in small increments, moving the dog closer to the stimulus (or the stimulus closer to your dog), obtaining your CER consistently at each new distance.
10. When your dog is happy to have higher intensity stimulus close to her, you're ready for the final phase. Return to the

original distance and obtain your CER there with a full intensity stimulus—a running, moving vacuum; multiple children laughing and playing; a tall man with a beard wearing a hat, sunglasses, and a backpack. Then gradually decrease the distance until your dog is happy to be in the presence of your full-intensity stimulus. She now thinks the stimulus is a very good thing, as a reliable predictor of very yummy treats. In the case of a human stimulus, you can gradually work up to actual interaction with the human(s) at this stage, by having the person(s) drop treats as they walk by, then letting her take treats from their fingers (no direct eye contact and no petting yet!), eventually working up to normal interaction.

Counter-conditioning is a very useful protocol that can work to change your dog's association with everything from handling (vet exams, nail trimming, grooming) to other dogs and humans, moving objects (cars, motorcycles, joggers), sounds (dogs on TV, doorbells, lawn mowers) and more.

*Counter-conditioning touch for eventual nail trimming.*

## Operant-conditioning

Operant-conditioning is another basic element of the science of behavior and learning. It says that all living things repeat behaviors that have 'good' consequences and avoid behaviors that have 'bad' outcomes; your dog makes deliberate behavior choices based on consequences. While B.F. Skinner is the most widely known scientist for his work with Operant-conditioning, there are many behavioral scientists who have contributed to this field of knowledge. Your dog is operating on her environment: "If I sit I will get a treat, therefore I will *choose* to sit!" She *makes* the treat happen by sitting.

*Look Ma, I can sit to make you give me a treat!"*

There are four principles of Operant-conditioning, often called "Quadrants." The terms used for these can be confusing. In general, we think of "positive" as meaning a good thing, and "negative" as meaning a bad thing—just as they are used with Classical-conditioning. But in Operant-conditioning they are used like mathematical terms—"Positive" means something is added, and "Negative" means something is taken away. "Reinforcement" simply means the behavior increases, and "Punishment" simply means the behavior decreases—it does not have to mean hitting or shocking the dog.

| **R+**<br>**Positive Reinforcement**<br>**Adding** an appetitive stimulus as a consequence to **increase** the likelihood that the behavior will occur in the future. | **P+**<br>**Positive Punishment**<br>**Adding** an aversive stimulus as a consequence to **decrease** the likelihood that the behavior will occur in the future. |
|---|---|
| **R-**<br>**Negative Reinforcement**<br>**Removing** an appetitive stimulus as a consequence to **decrease** the likelihood that the behavior will occur in the future. | **P-**<br>**Positive Punishment**<br>**Removing** an aversive stimulus as a consequence to **decrease** the likelihood that the behavior will occur in the future. |

## The four principles of Operant-conditioning are:

**Positive Reinforcement (R+)**—the dog's behavior makes a good thing happen (a good thing is added—positive), so the behavior increases (reinforcement): he sits, and you give him a treat. He likes getting treats (R+), so he sits more. All living things repeat behaviors that make good stuff happen!

We use R+ the most in force-free/positive reinforcement training.

**Negative Punishment (P-)**—the dog's behavior makes a good thing go away (negative), so the behavior decreases (punishment)—we don't want our good stuff to go away! When your dog jumps up to grab the ball from your hand, you hide the ball behind your back

(P-). He doesn't want the ball to go away, so he jumps up less. Then when he sits you throw the ball (R+). He learns that sitting makes the ball happen, so he sits more and jumps up less. Negative punishment works best if you follow it with positive reinforcement for the behavior you want instead.

Many force-free/positive trainers do use Negative Punishment occasionally in training. It is important that it not be accompanied by any verbal or body language aversives.

**Negative Reinforcement (R-)**—the dog's behavior makes a bad thing go away (negative). Your dog barks when the mail carrier drops mail through the slot. Then the mail carrier (bad thing) goes away, so over time the barking increases (reinforcement). Your dog doesn't know the carrier was going to go away anyway!

This can be used very carefully in force-free/positive training, if the "bad thing" is presented at a level that is not stressful to the subject. Using the Constructional Aggression Treatment protocol (CAT) developed by Kellie Snider, I "tamed" my feral barn cats— I fed them, waited for them to start eating, then took a step toward them. If they stopped eating, I stood still, and when they started eating again I moved away. In this case I was telling them that relaxing made the bad thing (me) go away, and eventually they became relaxed about my presence and no longer needed me to go away. I was no longer a bad thing … yay! Of course, it didn't hurt that I always brought food, which gave them a positive classical association with my arrival.

Kellie's book *Turning Fierce Dogs Friendly: Using Constructional Aggression Treatment to Rehabilitate Aggressive and Reactive Dogs* is available at Dogwise.com.

**Positive Punishment (P+)**—the dog's behavior makes a bad thing happen, so the behavior decreases: he jumps up and you knee him in the chest. He doesn't like a knee in the chest (it hurts!), so he jumps up less. This also carries the risk of injury to the dog and damaging the relationship between dog and human. I do not recommend deliberately using Positive Punishment when training your dog. Ever.

Because training methods that involve intimidation, coercion and physical force can cause undesirable side effects, including fear and aggression, positive trainers and other force-free animal care professionals primarily use Positive Reinforcement, secondarily Negative Punishment. Use Negative Reinforcement very sparingly, and do not use Positive Punishment. On those occasions where Negative Reinforcement may seem appropriate, it should be used as gently as possible, avoiding a strong response from the dog. Positive Reinforcement is without a doubt the best way to go!

## Enrichment

Another important facet of our dogs' lives, and of our examination of cognition, is enrichment. Canine enrichment has become a popular hashtag on social media, but it is more than stuffing a Kong or feeding your dog their kibble in a Snuffle Mat or Slow Feeder Bowl. Enrichment means acknowledging that dogs have species-specific and breed-specific needs. Finding a way to meet those needs can make training easier and fun. What a Border Collie finds enriching is going to be different than what a Bloodhound does!

For a deep dive into the fourteen categories of enrichment, read Allie Bender and Emily Strong's book *Canine Enrichment for the Real World* and the companion workbook, which are both available at Dogwise.com.

Now that you have an understanding of Operant and Classical-conditioning, let's get back to the fun of cognition!

# Part 2

# Cognition and Training

To set yourself (and your dog!) up for success, there are a number of basic skills you both will need in order to play Cognition/Brain Candy Games together. These are covered in the following chapters:

- Chapter 5—Operant-conditioning skills
- Chapter 6—Targeting
- Chapter 7—Waiting

If you already have experience with basic training skills like marking, shaping, capturing, and luring, and your dog has mastered targeting and has a solid "Wait!" behavior, then skip ahead to the Brain Candy games which begins in Chapter 8 on page 55. Either path you choose, just like a human version of Sniffari. Let the fun and learning begin!

If you want to test out cognition and find your dog's baseline, before diving into training, you can do some of these tests at home with your own dog to evaluate her cognitive abilities! These tests require little to no training and will give you a baseline of information as you dive into the canine cognition games that appear later in this book. Check out Dognition.com for more information.

# Chapter 5

# Operant-Conditioning Skills

---

Remember in Chapter 4 where I mentioned that I prefer using Operant-conditioning in my training practice? I believe that it is the key to harnessing the cognitive power of dogs to learn new and fun behaviors. Instead of just reacting, Operant-conditioning requires the dog to think! This is not a new idea. One of the early proponents of clicker training, Gail Fisher, wrote a book called *The Thinking Dog: Crossover to Clicker Training* back in 2009. While there are now many books on clicker training available, Fisher's emphasis on the dog having to think is important to keep in mind as we review some of the techniques that you can use in the games and exercises in the remainder of the book.

## Clicker/marker training

We said before that the dog needs to offer a behavior in order for Operant-conditioning to occur. How does the dog know which of many behaviors she tries is the one you want her to do? You communicate by "marking" the behavior as it occurs or as soon as possible afterwards. This can be a marker word like "yes," or a non-verbal distinct sound. Many trainers recommend using a **clicker**, a small handheld device used to communicate with our dogs that they have done exactly what we are looking for. Clickers are precise and consistent, which makes them a valued tool among many trainers. Think of a clicker like a shutter on a camera.

## Reward delivery and placement

Once you have chosen how you want to mark desirable behaviors, you will want to reward the dog as quickly as possible after it occurs. Usually this means a small food treat or something else the dog likes. Verbal praise can work; you can be creative about this as long as what you do helps build the behavior. With treats, placing them where the dog can get to them quickly is ideal.

## Shaping

**Shaping**, or as it's formally known, "shaping by successive approximations," simply means breaking down a behavior into tiny increments and reinforcing the dog at each step until you've achieved the full behavior. Some trainers believe that shaping is the ultimate approach to operant training and that any steps that stray off the pure shaping path are detrimental to ultimate results. Others incorporate shaping as I do—as a valuable part of a multi-faceted training program.

## The science behind shaping behavior

Shaping is a cognitive skill because it requires your dog to solve problems. It goes beyond simple Operant-conditioning because the dog must figure out the next step, not just repeat what has been previously reinforced. "What do I need to do *next*," she thinks, "to make the clicker click?" While you can use a verbal marker to let the dog that she has earned a treat, a clicker makes a sharp "Click" sound which many trainers prefer because the sound is consistent and it is more often more precise timing-wise (if your timing is off, the dog may not know what he did to earn the reward!). The shaping process works because behavior is variable. In any series of repetitions of a behavior your dog will give you variations in the manner that the behavior is performed—faster/slower, bigger/smaller, higher/lower, harder/softer, etc. When you are shaping, you are taking advantage of those variations of behavior that move you toward your final behavior goal.

Shaping has a number of important and useful applications and benefits for all kinds of training, including:

- Accomplishing a behavior that your dog finds physically difficult or confusing, such as a teaching a Greyhound to sit.
- Encouraging your dog to perform a behavior that she finds mentally difficult or confusing, such as teaching a crate-wary dog to enter her artificial doggie den.
- Fine-tuning a behavior your dog can already do, such as teaching fast, straight, close sits.
- Helping your dog learn how to offer behaviors, try new things and think creatively in order to solve problems, through shaping games such as in the 101 Things to Do With a Box shaping game described later in the chapter.
- Teaching your dog to do complex behaviors that would be very difficult or impossible to lure such as standing on his front paws and moving his hind feet up a wall to do a handstand.

One of the advantages of shaping behaviors is that it gives your dog agency (choice and control). If he's not comfortable entering the crate, he gets to choose whether to go any closer to it—or not. You can make good use of shaping with many of the cognition games that follow in this book.

## Shaping techniques

There are several ways to shape a behavior. You can use "lure/prompt shaping" as a sort of hybrid technique: you're still showing the dog what you want him to do by luring with a treat or prompting with a target or other body language. The shaping part comes in because you mark and reward small steps (successive approximations) as you lure and reinforce increments of progress to the final behavior. Imagine what the finished behavior looks like and then think of all the steps between the beginning and end of the behavior. Those in-between steps are the ones you will click and treat as your dog works towards the completed behavior. Dogs in our basic good manners classes are often taught the "Down" with lure-shaping by luring the dog's nose toward the floor with a treat, clicking and rewarding as the dog makes gradual progress toward the floor with his nose or other body parts.

Shaping "purists" tend to scoff at lure/prompt shaping and even accuse it of being a little coercive, but it can be very effective at getting behaviors more quickly, although perhaps slower at teaching dogs to think creatively and offer behaviors freely.

You can use "pure shaping," where you have a goal behavior in mind and without any prompting, reinforce small increments that the dog offers, such as described above for a faster sit. You can "free shape"—by doing training exercises without any preconceived notion of where you want the behavior to go. Free shaping is sometimes the most difficult concept for novice trainers, who are often legitimately perplexed by the idea of training without knowing what behavior you're trying to train until the dog chooses a behavior that you like and reward him.

## Lure/prompt shaping

**"Lure/prompt" shaping** can be used to quickly get a new behavior; however, it doesn't require the dog to figure out for himself what exactly it is that you want, which would be more cognitive. There are times when we deliberately set cognition aside and go with what's going to work best for the dog and his human in the moment.

Greyhounds are notoriously difficult to teach to sit. Theories abound as to why this is so; one theory has to do with the Greyhound's unique anatomy—a body shape that makes sitting an uncomfortable position. It's also possible that racing Greyhounds have been punished for sitting at the starting gate (because you don't want a dog sitting when the gates open!) and now are afraid to sit. Whatever the reason, it does seem that while most dogs offer sits easily, these long, lean, muscular dogs are often somewhat reluctant to do it.

To lure-shape a sit in a reluctant sitter, hold a treat at the tip of your dog's nose and lift it up slightly. If he lifts his nose to follow the tidbit, click and treat. Repeat this step by lifting the treat slightly higher and a little bit back over the head.

When each step seems easy for the dog, progress a little farther, continuing to move the treat up over the head. At the same time, watch for a bend in the hind legs. Be sure to click the slightest bend in the hocks, and when you start getting a consistent bend in the hocks, even a small one, keep luring but only click the leg bend, not the head lifts. You can also take a step back away from the dog and move the treat toward your chest. Reinforce gradually deeper bends in the legs until the dog is sitting.

Other dogs may have other reasons for failing to catch on quickly. A case in point is a shelter dog I saw in my Intern Academy last summer—a beautiful English Pointer who had been purchased for hunting trial work but was disqualified from competition due to a minor congenital rib deformity. At age four he had never been asked to sit and just didn't seem to understand what we were asking of him. In fact, he was the classic example of a shut-down dog—unwilling to offer any behavior at all. It took four days of the six-day academy, but on Thursday when his trainer finally got him to sit using lure-shaping, the whole class applauded wildly. Best of all, the dog got it! His eyes lit up and he proudly offered to sit after sit after sit after sit. In the remaining two days of the course, he and his trainer caught up on all the lessons that had been on hold while they worked on the sits, and both graduated with flying colors and big smiles.

Why not just push the dog into a sit or "tuck" him into a sit by pressing in gently above the hocks? Some trainers do teach the sit successfully in this manner. However, some dogs are reluctant to sit due to back or joint pain and need to learn to find a way to move into a sit that doesn't hurt; your push may cause excruciating pain. Others will simply push back when you push—a phenomenon known as the **opposition reflex**. Still others may resist and become aggressive when you try to physically force them to do something. That may or may not be the reason I had a recent client whose Scottish Terrier caused serious injuries to his prior trainer when she tried to push him into a sit. He resisted her first two push-sit attempts and on the third try he went up her arm with his teeth.

Several recent studies show that using coercion can actually damage the relationship between you and your dog. Perhaps the best reason of all to not use coercion!

## Free shaping

Free shaping is great for encouraging a dog who is somewhat shut down to offer behaviors, because she can't be wrong. Anything she does that even remotely relates to the exercise gets clicked and treated. And it's a great game to play with any dog to build a larger repertoire of behaviors for her to choose from. Once your dog is easily offering random behaviors you can, if you choose, switch to basic shaping with a goal behavior. A couple of my favorite fun free-shaping games to play with your dog are 101 Things and Body Parts, both described below and on the next page.

**101 Things to do with a ...**

You can use any old cardboard box for this, or it doesn't even have to be a box! You can play "101 Things to Do" with anything. We have used a small child's toy grocery cart, a rocking Mickey Mouse, a Winnie-the-Pooh on wheels and many more items gleaned from yard sales.

Your dog can be on leash, or off leash if she will stay and keep working with you. Stand or sit a few feet back from the box or object and just wait. You're looking for tiny pieces of behavior to click and treat—any tiny behavior that relates to the box—a look, a lean, a step, a sniff, a push. Remember that you have no specific goal in mind and you're not building up to a behavior—random behaviors are the goal.

If your dog gets hung up on one particular behavior, you can stop clicking that one and wait for something else. My rule is no more than three clicks in a row for the same behavior, then wait for something different. (Note: sniffing one point on the box is a different behavior from sniffing a different point on the box.) Look for behaviors involving different body parts—a glance of the eyes, the lean of a shoulder, the step of a paw, the sniff of the nose ... The more confident your dog is about offering behaviors the more easily you can just quit clicking one thing and wait for another.

At some point after your dog is offering *many* different behaviors, if you wish, you can decide on a goal behavior based on the ones your dog has offered and shape it into something specific—only front feet in the box; only hind feet in the box; all four feet in the box; turn the box over; fetch the box, stand on the box, or ...? But don't be in a hurry to do this—remember that the goal is to develop a large repertoire of behaviors your dog will offer when you're trying to shape a complex behavior.

*101 Things to do With a Box.*

## Body parts shaping

Body parts shaping helps your dog learn to offer behavior and it also helps you realize how precise this process can be for shaping the tiniest of movements for specific body parts—a nose, a paw, an ear, etc. When I was visiting the Taronga Park Zoo in Sydney, Australia, the animal caretakers proudly showed off their Sun Bear who had dental problems. They had body-shaped him to open his mouth and rest his teeth on the bars of his cage so they could examine his teeth without having to sedate him. Impressive!

## Here's how to shape body parts

Does your dog get stressed when you grasp her paw for a nail trim? For some dogs the stress is about the paw-holding, not the actual clipping! Use shaping to get her to rest her paw on a stool and keep it there. Then see if you can clip her nails without having to hold her paw. This worked beautifully for my Corgi, Lucy!

Sit in a chair with your dog facing you and watch your dog closely for a movement in one of her body parts. Even a tiny movement will do. For example, you could watch for a flick of her ear, a turn of her head, the lift of a paw, a tongue flick, or some other movement.

When you have captured one of these movements with your click and treat, that's the one you'll continue to focus on. Sit and wait for another movement of that same body part. Click and treat. Your goal is to reinforce that accidental behavior until your dog begins deliberately offering it. When she does, you can name it and incorporate it into a trick routine or keep working with it to shape it into something bigger if you choose.

## Pure shaping

Some trainers profess to teach their entire entry-level classes using pure shaping only. I'll admit I'm not that brave, but we do introduce the concept of basic shaping with our "Go to Your Place" exercise. I explain to my class that shaping is a Zen exercise—that it takes patience and close observation and that we'll be **splitting** behavior rather than lumping. **Lumping** means to reinforce large chunks of behavior—capturing a sit, for example. In contrast, splitting means to look for the tiniest piece of movement, click and reinforce that and *very slowly* build toward the final behavior. Splitting is the essence of shaping.

To shape a Go to Your Place behavior for example, set out a carpet square, dog bed, or blanket to designate the place you want her to go. You can do this without a physical object to mark the place but it's easier for canines and humans to succeed with a visual marker—and then you can generalize the behavior easily by moving the marker to another spot.

Now stand back several feet from the carpet square and watch your dog very closely. You're going to click and treat the tiniest motion toward where you want her to go—one step, a turn of the head, a flick of the ear. It doesn't even have to be directly toward the spot—in the general direction will do.

If you've already reinforced your dog consistently for offered behaviors, she'll probably catch on quickly. As she starts repeatedly making deliberate movements toward the rug to get clicked, you'll hold out slightly longer to build more behavior. Just slightly! You want her to get a little frustrated and try harder (harder = bigger behavior) but if you hold out for too long, she may give up and quit offering behavior altogether—you've inadvertently **extinguished** the behavior. After one or two 'hold-outs,' go back and click the previous step several times so she gets to succeed and will continue working, then try holding out again.

As she gets closer to the mat, you can move forward with her in order to keep delivering treats. Do not move ahead of her—that would be luring or prompting!

When she reaches the mat, reset. Move yourself and your dog several feet back and start again. You can invite your dog to move with you or, if preferred, lure with a treat or toss a treat to get her to move. The goal remains to shape her to go to the mat, not just to be on the mat. When she offers to go to the mat easily, start shaping her to lie down on it. Then work on duration and relaxation. The value of this exercise is to be able to park your dog there for a while. When she's consistently offering to go lie down on her mat, you can add the verbal "Go to Your Place!" cue.

**Your shaping session might look like this:**

1. Dog looks at mat. Click and treat.
2. Dog leans toward mat. Click and treat.
3. Dog takes a step towards mat—or even a half step/tiny step. Click and treat. (Toss the treat away from the mat so she can step toward the mat again.) Repeat multiple times.
4. Dog takes two steps toward mat. Again, click and toss treat away from mat. Repeat multiple times.

5. Dog takes three steps toward mat. Click, and toss treat away from mat. Repeat multiple times.
6. Continue with additional steps toward mat until dog is walking to mat from a distance away with each repetition.
7. Dog puts a paw on the mat. Click and toss treat away. Repeat multiple times, sometimes reinforcing a lower criterion.
8. Dog puts one paw on the mat. Click and treat. Occasionally hold out for more.
9. Dog puts two paws on the mat. Click and toss treat away. Repeat multiple times, sometimes reinforcing a lower criterion.
10. Dog puts two paws on the mat. Occasionally hold out for more.
11. Dog puts one or two paws further on the mat. Click and treat occasionally hold out for more.
12. Dog puts two paws further on the mat. Hold out. Click and toss treat away. Repeat multiple times, sometimes reinforcing a lower criterion.
13. Dog puts three paws on the mat. Click and toss treat away. Repeat multiple times, sometimes reinforcing a lower criterion.
14. Dog puts all four paws on the mat. Click and treat on the mat. Then toss treat away and repeat multiple times, sometimes reinforcing a lower criterion.
15. Dog sits on the mat. Click and treat on the mat. Then toss treat away and repeat multiple times, sometimes reinforcing a lower criterion.
16. Now start shaping for increased duration.

If your dog doesn't offer behaviors easily, it may take longer to shape the Place behavior. Be patient and remember to split—look for the tiniest of movement to reinforce. If she wants only to gaze adoringly into your eyes, look at the rug instead of her. If she just lies down at your feet for a snooze or gives up for lack of reinforcement, invite her back to her feet, reposition her and look for movement to reinforce as she repositions. The more you can find to reinforce, the less likely she is to lie down for another nap.

**Dubhy's Picnic: Using pure shaping to open the basket**

I decided to shape Dubhy to flip open a picnic basket with his nose. Because I'm doing basic shaping with a behavior goal in mind (not free shaping) I wouldn't click random offered behaviors that aren't in the shaping plan.

Here are the steps of my shaping plan. **Note that I would click and treat several times at each step**, unless Dubhy took a quantum leap over several steps in which case I'd be prepared to leap with him. After each step toward the basket, I toss the treat behind him so he can repeat that same step again.

1. Looks at basket.
2. Leans toward basket.
3. Moves a small step toward basket.
4. Moves another step toward basket.
5. Repeat Step 4 until he is at the basket.
6. Sniffs basket.
7. Sniffs basket closer to basket lid corner where the opening is.
8. Repeat Step 7 until he is sniffing at the opening.
9. Sniffs basket at basket lid corner.
10. Nudges lid corner (here I might need to hold out to wait for stronger behavior to get the nudge).
11. Nudges lid corner harder.
12. Nudges hard enough to move lid corner.
13. Nudges hard enough to lift up lid corner.
14. Nudges hard enough to lift lid corner higher.
15. Nudges hard enough to flip lid open—VOILA!!!!!

When I put my plan into action and began training Dubhy to flip open the basket, I chose to take a short-cut and do a little prompting with a target stick. That allowed us to skip steps 1-4 and go directly to step 5, sniffing the basket lid corner. From there it only took a few minutes for Dubhy to repeatedly offer a strong, reliable "open the basket" behavior.

Now that we have reliability with the goal behavior of opening the basket, I could incorporate it into a trick routine—perhaps packing picnic supplies into the basket or unpacking them and laying them out on a waiting picnic blanket. Or perhaps he could find a small "lost" dog who was trained to lie quietly hidden in the basket. Or ... we're off to see the wizard?

Dedicated pure shapers will write out their complete shaping plan, considering each potential step in the process and measuring their progress against the written plan. Less scientifically disciplined trainers may work with just a mental picture of their shaping plan. You can do each shaping session for as long or as short as you like. Assuming your dog is happy to play the game, you can keep on playing! As with all training, try to end the session while your dog is still enthusiastic and successful.

*I also used Shaping to teach Dubhy to play the piano.*

I really came to appreciate the power of shaping when I first purchased agility equipment, set it up in the backyard, and ran to get Dubhy to see what he'd do with it. To my delight, as I introduced him to each piece of equipment, he immediately started doing stuff—sniffing it, pawing at it, biting it, jumping on it, just trying out different things to see what he needed to do to get me to click. Made training a breeze!

# Chapter 6
# Targeting

---

A great way to practice your shaping skills is by teaching your dog how to target, or touch one of his body parts to an object. This will help both you and your dog in the Brain Candy Games section of the book including:

- Indication behavior (Chapter 9)
- Hit a button (Chapter 12)
- Chin Rest (Chapter 14)

You can teach your dog to **paw targe**t, place his paw somewhere specific, or to **nose target**, touch or push an object with his nose. A chin rest is another variation of the targeting behavior. The applications for teaching your dog to target are endless! You may find that your dog prefers targeting with his paws over his nose, so I recommend having separate cues for each behavior.

## How to teach your dog to target

If you offer the open palm of your hand to your dog with your fingers pointed toward the floor at nose level or below, most dogs will stretch forward and sniff it. Mark with your clicker or verbal marker and give your dog a treat. Repeat several times and you're on your way! If your dog needs a little encouragement to touch, you can rub a bit of a tasty treat on your hand and when she sniffs or licks it, mark and treat. You can also try backing up a few steps and invite your dog to follow you—getting her to move will often free her up to nose-touch your hand. Most dogs learn to touch the proffered palm within just a few tries.

As with all the behaviors we teach, as soon as you can predict that your dog is going to touch your palm with her nose when you offer it, begin using the verbal cue. I use "Touch!" Note that if she already thinks an open palm is the cue to offer her paw to you for a "Shake" then you can offer a closed fist, the back of your hand or two fingers in place of the open palm.

When your dog is eagerly touching her nose to your hand, start moving your hand to different locations, so she realizes that "Touch!" is a 'moving' exercise. Now generalize the target behavior to other objects. I like to start with a wooden spoon, short ruler, or target stick—I can hold my hand near the very end of the stick so when she goes to touch my hand, she also touches the stick. I gradually push the stick farther and farther through my hand and only click if she touches the end of the stick, not my hand. You can then use the stick as a pointer if needed to show her what you want her to touch. I will still ask her to touch my hand sometimes—but make a clear difference between asking her to touch my hand, the stick, or some other object as described above. The offering or indication of the target object is key to her understanding what you want her to touch and that you still always want her to wait for that "Touch!" cue.

# Chapter 7

## But First, Wait!

---

To succeed with discrimination (aka "stimulus discrimination"), your dog needs to have a solid Wait or Stay behavior in addition to the Target indicator behavior discussed in the previous chapter. He must be able to wait when you present the item and name it for him and not leap to touch it until you give the "Touch!" cue.

While some people may use the "Wait" and "Stay" cues interchangeably, I find there is real value in making a distinction between the two. In my dogs' world "Stay" means stay in the exact position I left you (usually a sit or a down) until I ask you to get up, while "Wait" just means pause. I actually use the "Wait" cue a whole lot more than I do the "Stay" cue in everyday life. In fact, it's probably one of my most-used cues.

Perhaps I'm heading out to meet a client. I say "Wait" as I open the back door to tell my dogs Sunny, KC and Kai they aren't going with me, but they are free to move around the house. If I said "Stay" I would technically be asking them to freeze and not move until I return two hours later. I may have well-trained dogs but that's not going to happen!

My favorite way to teach the wait behavior is to teach a wait for the food bowl and then generalize the behavior to other situations. Here's how to train it:

1. At mealtime, have your dog sit by his feeding location, and tell him "Wait!" Hold his bowl at your shoulder level, off to one side so you won't be lowering it directly under his nose, then click (or use a verbal marker of your choice), take a treat out of the food bowl and feed it to him. Don't lower the bowl yet, just hold it still and mark and reward him for not moving from his sitting position. If he loves his regular food, you can use that to treat after you mark. If he's not wildly enthusiastic about it, use higher value treats that you've put into his food bowl with his food. If he gets up before you click, give a cheerful "Oops … Sit!" cue and try again. If he gets up after you click and treat, just ask him to sit and wait again before the next repetition. Repeat several times, cuing him "Wait" for each repetition.
2. Now with the bowl at shoulder level, tell him "Wait," then lower the bowl a few inches. If he remains sitting, click your clicker or use your verbal marker, and quickly raise the bowl back up after you click. Take a treat out of the food bowl and feed it to him. If he gets up when you lower the bowl, do another cheerful "Oops … Sit!" and try again, this time only lowering it a fraction of an inch.
3. Gradually lower the bowl a bit more, still starting at shoulder level, telling him "Wait" each time, with several successful repetitions at each new position before going lower. If you get two errors in a row, you've gone too quickly; go back to the last bowl position where he was successful and proceed more slowly with your bowl lowering.
4. When you get the bowl all the way to the floor without him moving, set it down, click, and pick it back up before giving your dog the treat. Repeat several times, telling him "Wait" each time. (Be ready to raise it back up quickly if he tries to go for it!)
5. Next, when you get the bowl to the floor, click but leave the bowl on the floor while you feed him the treat. Repeat several times, telling him "Wait" each time.
6. Finally, tell him "Wait," set the bowl on the floor, click and treat, and tell him, "Okay, you can have it!" After all, it *is* breakfast time!

*Teaching "Wait"*

## More good reasons to teach a wait behavior

Circumstances arise every day where "Wait" comes in very handy:

**Wait at the door**: It's important for your dog to learn that an open door doesn't mean he gets to go running out, but rather that he needs to wait for an invitation. Start with him sitting at the door, ask him to wait and reach a few inches toward the doorknob. If he stays sitting, click and treat. If not, "Oops" and start over with even less of a reach toward the door. When he is successful, gradually reach closer to the doorknob, eventually jiggling it, then opening the door a crack, then a bigger crack until you can step outside without him following you. If you are going to invite him to come through a doorway after a "Wait" cue, use a release cue, like "Free!" or "Go ahead!" so he knows when it's okay to exit.

**Wait in the car**: Using the same steps as used to teach your dog to wait at the door, practice waiting in the car, so he also understands that an open car door is not an invitation to jump out. This can be especially useful if your car ever breaks down on a busy highway. (Crates and seat belts are the best approach to keeping your dog safe in your car.)

**Wait on a hike**: You can also use the "Wait" cue to ask your dog to pause if he's wandering too far ahead of you when you're on an off-leash outing. I use this frequently on our around-the-farm hikes. After hearing the "Wait" cue, my dogs pause for several seconds, then continue their hiking fun. If I need a longer pause, I just cue it again.

**Wait to greet**: If your dog is very friendly and eager to dash up to greet that dog on the path ahead (or perhaps a senior citizen in the park) who looks less-than-enthused about a nose-to-nose encounter, then a well-trained wait behavior will pause your dog long enough to let you grasp his collar, attach your leash, and orchestrate appropriate greetings or no greetings.

**Wait for the leash**: Because a leash is such reliable predictor of walks, lots of dogs get quite excited when their human picks it up. Ask your dog to "Sit" and "Wait" for the leash. If he jumps up when you pick it up say "Oops," set the leash down, and ask him to sit and wait again. Repeat until he will remain seated and waits until his leash is attached.

**Wait, It's a Game!** Everything's more fun if we make it a game, right? With your dog on leash, run with him a few steps then say "Wait!" and stop moving. When he stops, pause several seconds, then say, "Let's go!" and take off running again. Encourage him to get excited! Then say "Wait!" and stop again. Vary the amount of time you pause so he never knows when the "Let's go!" is coming. When he's really good at stopping on your "Wait!" cue, try it off-leash running next to him (in a fenced area at first, if needed) and eventually when he's farther and farther away from you.

By the way, my Kelpie, Kai, did a brilliant "Wait" one morning when he was sitting in the barnyard and a bunny dashed toward him. I said "Wait" and Kai didn't move as the bunny noticed Kai, did a backflip and darted past him just two feet away. Good boy Kai!

# Chapter 8

# Shape, Color and Object Discrimination Brain Candy Games

---

**Key cognitive processes for improved and enhanced learning:**

- **Perceiving**
- **Recognizing**
- **Volition**
- **Conceiving**
- **Discriminating**
- **Reasoning**
- **Memory**
- **Learning**

The fast-mapping object identification skill demonstrated so aptly by Chaser under the tutelage of retired psychologist Dr. John Pilley was only the beginning of our appreciation for canine **discrimination** talents—albeit a Herculean-strong beginning. Dogs can be taught to demonstrate their abilities to distinguish between different shapes and colors, as well as objects not limited to their toys. It's an amazing talent and one you'll want to show off to your family and friends when you do demos at nursing homes, and maybe even on America's Got Talent! (And maybe Britain's Got Talent, Australia's Got Talent, Japan's Got Talent and more!)

## Object discrimination

Now that your dog has learned to wait on cue, we can start our discrimination games. We start with Object Discrimination because objects are the most **salient** (meaningful) to dogs. Then, after they've learned the *concept* of discrimination we can generalize it to the less salient targets. To start, you will need two objects. As Pilley suggested, toys are most likely to draw your dog's attention.

> **A note on choice of cues**
> I personally teach my dogs that an action cue is the release cue, but I realize that many people teach that their dog must wait for a trained release cue before they can move. As you progress through the steps below, if your dog is trained to only move if given a release cue after being told to "Wait" or "Stay," the order of cues should be: "Fido, Wait! Fuzzy (name the object), Touch (give the Targeting Indication cue), Okay!" (Or whatever your release cue is if it isn't "Okay!") You will always keep the "Touch" cue in the sequence, so your dog doesn't start to think the name of the object is the cue to touch.

Let's say you're going to use two toys named Fuzzy and Squeak.

1. Select two objects that your dog likes—a stuffed toy, a ball, a stick. If he already knows the names of the objects, you're ahead of the game!
2. Name one object—let's say it's "Fuzzy." Tell your dog to "Wait!" or "Stay!" and hold Fuzzy in front of you in your hand at your dog's nose level. If your dog moves, whisk Fuzzy behind you and remind your dog to "Wait." Bring Fuzzy out several times, using your wait cue each time, until you can bring it out and your dog doesn't move. Now cue your dog to "Wait," bring Fuzzy out at nose level, pause, and then cue him to touch it with his nose or paw (whichever you taught him)—i.e., "Fuzzy, touch!" When he moves his nose or paw to touch the object, mark and treat. (Put the item behind your back between repetitions.) Repeat several times until he is solid with his wait behavior and touches the object easily when given the cue.

3. Now do the same with your second object: "Wait, Squeak, Touch!" Mark and treat.
4. Next you will ask him to "Wait" and offer both objects at the same time. To help him succeed you will offset them so the one you are going to ask him to touch (Fuzzy) is significantly closer to him. Cue him to touch that one: "Fuzzy, Touch!" If he heads for the incorrect one, whisk it behind your back and wait for him to touch Fuzzy. Mark and treat. Repeat multiple times, randomly alternating which one you offer closer to him and cue him to touch. Also switch sides so the same object isn't always in the same hand.
5. Gradually decrease the offset of the target object until you can offer both to him at the same distance and he will consistently touch the one you cue him to touch.
6. Now repeat the process with the objects on the floor several feet away, with both of you facing the objects. Again, start with the target object closer to him to help him succeed, until he can touch either requested object consistently and correctly with both objects the same distance away—and then with the correct one even farther away.
7. Finally, name and add more objects to his repertoire. The sky's the limit!

*Teaching Object Discrimination.*

## Shape discrimination

For this one you will need to find or make shapes that are similar in size and color, with the shape being the only difference. In my group classes, we use black shape silhouettes (squares, circles, and triangles) glued onto square white boards.

1. As with the object discrimination game, ask your dog to "Wait!" then hold up one shape at nose level, name it, and ask your dog to touch it, i.e., "Square, touch!" (use your release cue if needed) and then mark and treat. Repeat several times until your dog touches the Square easily when asked.
2. Now do the same with your second shape—"Wait, Circle, Touch!" Mark and treat. Repeat until he touches the Circle easily when cued. (I don't use "Round" because it sounds too much like "Down.").

3. Now cue your dog to "Wait" and offer both shapes at the same time. Again, in order to help him succeed, offer one closer to him and cue him to touch that one. If he heads for the wrong one, whisk it behind your back and wait for him to touch the other one. Repeat multiple times, randomly alternating which one you offer closer to him and cue him to "Touch." Also switch sides so the same shape isn't always in the same hand.
4. Now repeat the process with the shapes on the floor propped up against boxes or stands of some sort, several feet in front of you and your dog, again starting with the target shape closer to him to help him succeed. Gradually reduce the offset until he can touch either requested shape consistently and correctly with both objects the same distance away—and then with the correct one even farther away.
5. Finally, name and add more shapes to his repertoire. Triangle? Hexagon? Even better… can you add silhouettes and have him identify the names of things? A dog or a horse? A bird? A tree? A house? Or …???

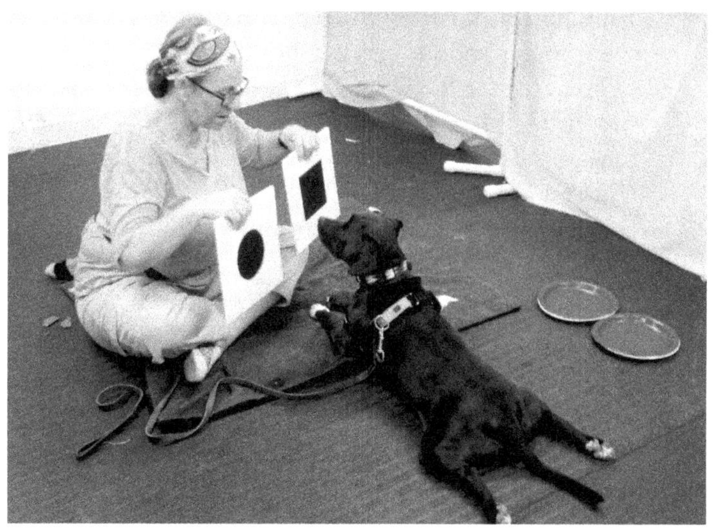

*Teaching Shape Discrimination.*

## Color discrimination

This one can be a little tricky because dogs are red-green color-blind like some humans. Blue looks like blue to them, yellow looks like yellow, and black looks like black. Greens and oranges also look yellowish while reds look brown or tan. In my classes, when we teach colors, we use colored paper plates. We always start with blue and yellow since we know dogs can distinguish those easily. We then use black for our third color and finally red, since whatever it looks like to the dog, we know it's different from blue, yellow or black. The process is essentially the same as the previous two discrimination exercises.

1. Cue your dog to "Wait," hold up one color at nose level, name it, and then cue your dog to touch it. For example, "Wait, Blue, Touch!" Mark and treat. Repeat several times until your dog touches it easily.
2. Now do the same with your second color. "Wait, Yellow, Touch!" then mark and treat.
3. Now ask your dog to "Wait" and offer both colors at the same time at nose level. To help him succeed, offer one closer to him and cue him to touch that one. Mark and treat. If he heads for the wrong one, whisk it behind your back and wait for him to touch the other one. Repeat multiple times, randomly alternating which one you offer closer to him and ask him to touch. Also switch sides so the same color isn't always in the same hand.
4. Now repeat the process with the colors on the floor several feet in front of you and your dog, propped up against boxes or stands of some sort. Again, start with the target color closer to him to help him succeed, and gradually reduce the offset until he can touch either requested color consistently and correctly with both the same distance away.
5. Finally, name and add black and red to his repertoire.

*Teaching Color Discrimination.*

What then? You can get creative and mix them up. See if he can learn to select the black balls from a pile of yellow and blue ones. Teach him the names of the rooms in your house and ask him to bring the yellow Frisbee® to you from the bedroom. Teach him the names of family members and ask him to take the blue Teddy to Dad in the living room. And then?

# Chapter 9

## Match to Sample

## The "Same As" Brain Candy Game

---

**Key cognitive processes for improving and enhancing learning:**

- **Perceiving**
- **Recognizing**
- **Volition**
- **Conceiving**
- **Discriminating**
- **Problem solving**
- **Reasoning**
- **Learning**

### Who knew ...?

Match to Sample is one of my favorite cognition games because first, it's a real crowd pleaser and second, it is astoundingly easy. Who knew, indeed? The Same As concept simply means that your dog can identify (choose) and indicate to you which object (or objects) match the one you show her. Perhaps it shouldn't amaze us that our dogs are able to do this, but it does.

## Teaching Match to Sample

To teach Match to Sample you will need a collection of multiple identical objects: red plastic cups, water bottles, tennis balls, Kongs® (same size, same color) or multiples of anything else that strikes your fancy. While your dog's own toys may be more salient for her and therefore a little easier for her to pay attention to and match at first, she should in short order be able to correctly match any two or more items of your choice. I like to use a raised surface like a low stool as my "presentation platform" so your objects are clearly distinctive from anything else on the floor.

Your dog will need a strong **indication behavior.** Some trainers ask the dog to pick up the object. My preference is for a nose touch or paw touch. This gives you more versatility—the dog can touch objects with her nose or paw that might be too large, heavy or bulky for her to pick up, and/or that I might not want to be in my dog's mouth! Should you decide that you do want her to pick up some objects but not every one you match, you can teach her other verbs (Take! Fetch!) later. I like to use nose targeting for Match to Sample because dogs tend to investigate with their noses, making a nose touch an easy behavior to prompt and capture.

### Here's how to teach your dog to match:

Start with your dog sitting or lying down on a mat in front of your item presentation platform. Ask her to wait there, parked, until you give her the cue to indicate that you want her to match the object.

1. Have two identical objects. Place one on your platform.
2. Hold up the other object identical to the one on the platform and say "Same" (or "Match" or whatever you want your Match cue to be), say "Touch," then indicate the object on the platform. If your dog needs a release cue from her waiting position on the mat, say "Touch," then give her the release cue and indicate the object on the platform.
3. When she touches it, mark and treat. You may need to encourage her to touch the object the first few times until she realizes what you are asking her to do. You can indicate it with a finger point or with your target stick. You will fade

the indicator when she has grasped the concept; it shouldn't take long.

Repeat step three numerous times, until she easily touches the object on the platform when you say "Same." (You do not have to keep using the "Touch" cue and the indicator once she realizes that "Same" means touch the same object.)

4. Now place a second item (I call this the **distractor object**) on the platform several inches away from the object she has been touching on the platform in the prior steps.
5. Hold up your identical object and tell her "Same!" If she touches the incorrect (distractor) object just wait for her to touch the correct one, mark and treat. Do not give a verbal correction—let her think it through. Repeat until she touches the correct object at least 80% of the time. Be sure to switch the objects around every few repetitions so the correct object isn't always on the same side—we want to be sure she's not just showing a side preference.

*Teaching Match to Sample.*

## Stepping it up

You're ready to step it up a notch! Each time your dog consistently achieves 80% correctly, you're ready to move to the next step:

1. Pick a different pair of identical items and repeat the process so she realizes that other items can also match.
2. When she's got that right, add a distractor.
3. When she's doing well with one distractor add another, so you now have two distractors.
4. Now leave your two distractors down and pick a different pair of identical objects to match.
5. Try getting a little tricker—add another distractor but make it one of the objects you had previously matched.
6. Gradually add additional distractors until your dog can identify and match the object from as many as a half-dozen different distractors.

## The perfect match

Now you're ready for graduate level matching!! Try these variations and see how much of a genius your dog really is. Be sure to achieve consistent 80% success at each step before making it harder:

1. Place multiple items on the platform that all match the one in your hand. No distractors at first. See if she indicates two matches. Then try three. Repeat your "Same" cue and encourage her if necessary.
2. Once she is consistently successful 80% of the time, add a distractor. Then gradually add multiple distractors.
3. Next a tricky one ... place down two different match items that you have already used with her—perhaps a plastic cup and a water bottle. Hold up the first "same" object—a plastic cup—and ask her to match—to touch the cup on the platform.
4. Now go back to the beginning of the last step but this time add distractors.

5. Finally, include in your distractors some of the objects you previously asked her to match but don't match them this time—match to some of your other objects. As with each prior step, start with a smaller number of items to make it simpler for her and work up to more complicated/more difficult.

## The crowning glory

Are you ready for la pièce de résistance? The crowning glory? If you and your dog can achieve this one, you deserve a place in the canine hall of fame. . . . It has been done . . . but very few dogs that I know of have ever accomplished this one: Match to Sample from a *photograph*! Yes, from a picture. (If you do it you have to promise to let me know.)

The process is relatively simple, building on what you've already done. Take a nice, crisp, clear photo against a white background (or a dark background if the object is white) of the object you want your dog to match. Using the same setup as before, hold up the photo and give your "Same!" cue. Encourage your dog if she needs a little help at first to understand what you're asking of her. When she realizes that she is matching the object in the photo, start the process of slowly adding distractors. Include some other photos as distractors as well. Gradually increase the complexity of the matches as described in the other steps above. Just see how far you and your dog can go!

## Postscript

Here's an even wilder idea. This is one I have *never* heard of—although maybe it's been done and I just haven't heard of it . . . What if your dog could identify a *human* from a photograph? It would be the same process as above—you would need a sharp, clear photo of the human. Help your dog understand that you want her to indicate the human from the photo and then add distractor humans. What do you think?

"But, your honor, my dog knows how to identify humans from photographs, and she identified the defendant as the one who broke into my house and stole my TV and stereo system when I wasn't home!"

All I can say is, if you succeed in getting your dog to identify *humans* from photographs, I *really* want you to let me know!

# Chapter 10

# Choice and Consent Brain Candy Games

---

**Key cognitive processes for improving and enhancing training:**

- **Perceiving**
- **Volition**
- **Memory**
- **Discrimination**

## Brain Candy Game #1: You Choose

Now that we have come to understand the value of giving our dogs choice in their lives, how do we incorporate that into our relationships with them? We can introduce choice to our dogs by teaching them a "You Choose" cue and then look for occasions where we can let them know that they can make a choice. Here's how you can do this:

1. Select a very high-value treat. Show one to your dog and name it (Meat, Beef, Chicken, etc.). Let her eat it. Repeat several times.
2. Select a low-value treat. Show it to your dog and name it (Kibble, Milk bone, squeaky toy). Let her eat or chew it. Repeat several times. You are teaching her the names of the different treats so she can make an informed choice.

3. Now tell her to "Wait," and place your high-value treats in one bowl, your low-value treats in another bowl. (The bowls should look the same.) Hold the high value treat bowl in one hand and say its name. "Chicken!" Hold the low value treat bowl in your other hand and say its name. "Kibble."

*Name the objects as you show them to your dog.*

4. Show her each bowl again, naming them as you show them to her. Now place both bowls on the floor at the same time, at your feet, six inches apart with your dog two feet back, right in the center of the bowls. Repeat the "Wait" cue if needed to keep her from diving into the bowls. Your dog and the two bowls should form an equilateral triangle.
5. Now say "You Choose!" or "Pick One!" (or whatever you want your "You Choose" cue to be) and invite her to choose a bowl. Be sure you don't inadvertently point to either of the bowls! (Some dogs have been taught to stay in position until they are given a release cue. If this is the case with your dog, give your release cue *after* the "You Choose" cue.)

While she eats the treat from the bowl she chooses quickly, pick up the other bowl or toy. You want her to understand that there is an **opportunity cost**—when she chooses one treat it means she doesn't also get to eat the other treat.

*You Choose!*

*Note: If your dog is a significant food-guarder you can do this with two toys instead—one you know is a very favorite toy and one that she might be less excited about. Name the toys and place them on the floor using the same procedure described above or offer one in each hand. Or you can just choose to do it with toys instead of food if you prefer, even if your dog doesn't guard food. And if you offer the toys in your hands instead of placing them on the floor you can toss the one she chooses for a fun "Chase It!" game.*

Repeat numerous times, randomly switching which side contains the high-value/low-value treat or toy, until it's clear she's realizing she can choose her preference. Be sure to also mix up which treat or toy you name first—high-value sometimes, low-value sometimes. You might be surprised to discover what you *think* is higher value for her may not be! Remember, it's *her* choice, do not try to coax her to go for the one *you* think is higher value.

One of the many highlights of cognition training is getting to watch your dog's brain work. As you repeat the Choice Game (and many of the others in the pages that follow) you are likely to eventually see her thinking—glancing back and forth between both objects and making a very decided, deliberate choice. It's so cool!

Many dogs show a definite side preference—always picking the bowl on their left (or right) side regardless of which side her preferred treat is on. If your dog does this, you can take a time-out to teach her that both sides have value, then return to the You Choose game.

## Brain Candy Game #2: Righty/Lefty

If you see that your dog is always choosing the bowl on the same side regardless of which treat is in it, you probably have a dog with a strong side preference. Note that we label the side preference according to the *dog's* side—so if she always goes to *her* left, she has a left-side preference. If she goes to *her* right, she has a right-side preference. You can help her become an equal-opportunity side-chooser by doing this:

1. Take a very high-value treat, put it in the bowl, name it as you show her the bowl, tell her "Wait" and put it on the floor in front of you on her *less-preferred side.* If she has a right-side preference, put it on her left side. For a left-side preference put it on her right side. Say "You Choose" (even though she's not making a choice) and watch her go to the bowl.

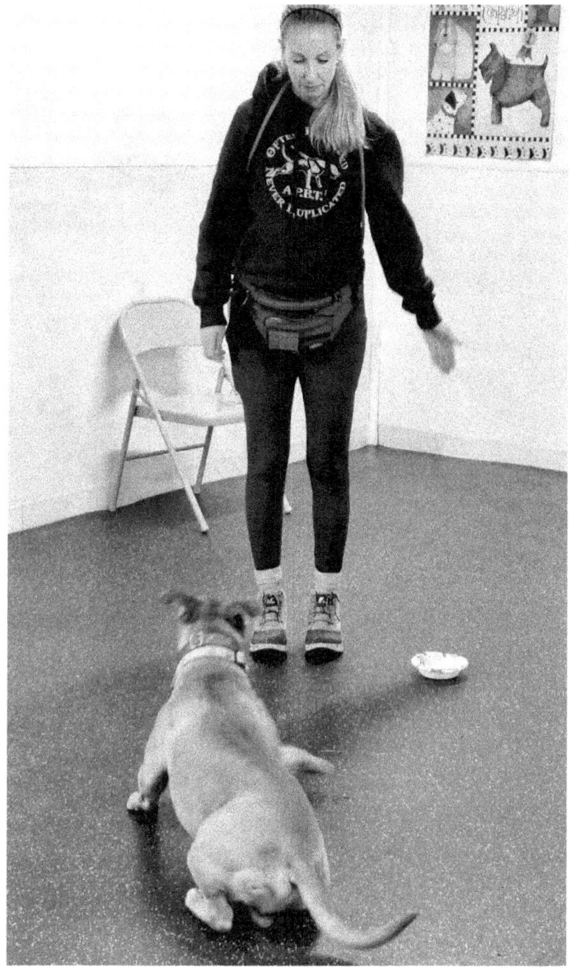

*Righty/Lefty—Put one bowl down.*

2. Repeat multiple times—a half-dozen or many more, depending on your dog's normal learning speed.
3. Now put your high value treat in one bowl and leave the other bowl empty. Show her each bowl and name it as you show it to her using your high value treat name and naming the other one "Empty." Tell her "Wait" and put both bowls down at the same time with the Empty bowl on her preferred side—but far off to the side, with the high-value bowl on her non-preferred side only slightly off-center.

*Righty/Lefty—Put two bowls down, far apart.*

4. If she goes for the empty bowl let her investigate, discover that it's empty, and return to eat the high-value treat. Repeat multiple times until she doesn't bother to investigate the empty bowl.
5. Gradually bring the empty bowl closer and closer until you are back to your equilateral triangle.
6. Now put your high-value treat in one bowl, your low-value treat in the other bowl. Show her each bowl and name it as you show it to her. Tell her "Wait" and put both bowls down at the same time with the low value treat on her preferred side—but once again *far* off to the side, with the high value bowl on her non-preferred side only slightly off-center.
7. If she goes to the high value bowl you're on your way! If she goes to the far-offset low-value bowl (Darn it!) you've moved forward too quickly—back up and repeat Steps 3 through 6.
8. When she is able to do Step 6, you can gradually bring the low-value bowl closer until you are back to equilateral and

then start switching sides, with the high-value bowl sometimes on her preferred side and sometimes on her less preferred side. Now she's really choosing!

*Righty/Lefty—put both bowls down closer together.*

## Brain Candy Game #3: Both sides now—Invite your dog to make a choice

Now that your dog understands the *concept* of choice, take some time to think of other ways you can invite your dog to make choices in her daily life:

- Go to the door and say, "Want to stay in or go out? You choose!"
- Offer her two of her toys and say, "Fluffy or Dino? You choose!"
- You're hiking in the woods and the trail divides. Say, "This way or that way? You choose!"
- "Your bed or the sofa? You choose!"
- Now think up more of your own—the more the better!

The more you do this the more she will be able to generalize the "Choice" concept to any situation where you offer it. Remember that if you do offer your dog a choice opportunity you *must* honor her choice and go with her decision—so don't ask unless you fully intend to let her make the choice!

## Brain Candy Game #4: Consent testing

Another way we can give a dog agency is by doing a **consent test**—asking permission to do things with her or to her. Petting is a great example. It's easy to assume that dogs love to be petted. After all, we love to pet them! In fact, some dogs *do* love being petted, scratched and even hugged. Others just tolerate it, but don't really enjoy it. Still others actively dislike it and either avoid it or let us know in no uncertain terms—with a growl, air snap or even a bite—clearly that means they aren't happy about intimate contact with humans.

In fact, there are probably more dogs who tolerate or actively dislike petting than dogs who really love it. Start watching more closely the interactions around you between dogs and humans. You may be surprised to realize how many dogs back up or duck away or don't really look happy when someone, even their very own human, reaches out to pet them!

Sadly, the ones who speak out about their discomfort with petting often get themselves in serious trouble. Dogs who growl, snap at or bite humans tend to have short lives. Yet, it's not their fault. Usually, well before a growl, snap or bite happens, the dog has given many body language signals asking the human to leave them alone. These include any social behavior related to fighting, mostly intended to avoid actual aggression, including threats, displays, retreats, placating, and conciliation. Unfortunately, many humans are very incompetent at reading canine body language. Can we say many humans honestly suck at it? Or worse, they just think they have the dog-given right to do anything they want to their dog regardless of how the dog feels about it? Newsflash—we don't. (See the discussion on body talk below.)

Hence, the creation of the consent test where we ask our dog if she wants to be petted. Here's how a consent test might look for petting:

- Sit down in an enclosed space with your dog off-leash. Be patient.
- Rest one open hand on your leg or lap, palm up. Ideally, the dog will approach you, but you can call her if necessary. No luring with treats allowed.
- When the dog approaches, initiate contact. The best first contact is usually a scratch on the chest. Do not pet the dog on top of her head.
- Use the three-second rule. Scratch/pet for three seconds then remove your hand. If the dog moves closer or nudges your hand and has a relaxed facial expression, she is inviting more attention. If she moves away, leans away, looks away or just remains neutral without interacting, she's saying, "No thanks!"
- Repeat several times, continuing to use the three-second rule. Dogs can change their minds, so even if your dog invited additional petting at first, be alert for signs that she has had enough and wants the petting to stop. (This is often when people get bitten—when they fail to notice the "all done" signs!)
- Repeat this process when allowing other people to pet your dog.

**Body talk: Signs that your dog enjoys petting**

- The dog asks to be petted by moving into your space, maybe even leaning on you
- She shoves nose or moves her whole body under your hand
- She pulls your hand toward her with a paw
- Her body is relaxed
- She does a happy-butt dance under your hand
- Her eyes get dreamy-droopy when she is petted
- She flops happily onto the floor while being petted (note that going "belly up" is sometimes an invitation to rub her tummy, and sometimes an appeasement behavior actually asking you to stop)
- She melts happily onto your lap while being petted

**Signs that your dog doesn't enjoy petting**

- The dog stands still but doesn't actively engage with you
- She ducks away when you reach for her
- Her body is tense
- She moves away from you
- She looks away (prolonged active avoidance, not just a quick glance away at some distraction)
- She yawns, scratches, licks her lips, pants, and/or exhibits other stress signals
- And, of course, anything more obvious like growling and snapping

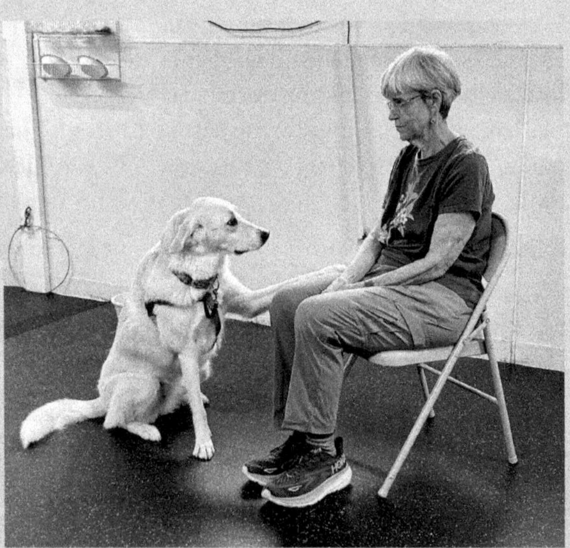

*Consent Testing—Does this dog want to be petted?*

## More on consent testing and rehabilitation

### Interacting with another dog

If two dogs are playing exuberantly and you're not sure one is having a good time, separate the dogs and move them about six feet apart. Restrain the more active dog and release the one you're not sure is enjoying the interaction. If that dog stays still or moves away, she's saying she's had enough. If she moves forward and re-engages with the other dog, she's saying yes, she wants to play more.

This is critically important for the well-being of the dog who is not enthusiastic about the play session. If she is not rescued from the play situation, the dog who really doesn't want to play ultimately may be pushed into defensive aggression just to save herself. The defensive dog then may be blamed for starting a fight and labelled as "dog-aggressive" (because *"she started it!"*) when it's the more exuberant player who is at fault for not honoring the defensive dog's signals that she really doesn't want to play.

### Participating in an activity

Invite your dog to walk toward a hospital (if she's a therapy dog), training or show grounds (for a competition dog), etc. Ask her if she wants to go for a walk or play in the yard. If she moves eagerly forward, you're good to go. If she shows any reluctance to move, moves with tension, or exhibits stress signals for anything you invite her to do, you may want to rethink that activity or start a rehabilitation process.

### Rehabilitating consent

If your dog tells you she doesn't want to participate in an activity that you had your heart set on, you have a couple of options.

You may be able to slowly and carefully work to rehabilitate her association with the activity to help her love it as much as you do. First have a thorough medical checkup to be sure there's not a physical reason (pain) for your dog's reluctance to engage with hospital patients, run fast, jump over jumps or whatever you're asking her to do. If her vet check is clear, start incorporating small bits of the activities into other venues that your dog really loves.

The pain piece is critically important. Many years ago, I was showing my first Pomeranian, Dusty, in AKC obedience competitions. We had earned our CD (Companion Dog) title and were working on our CDX (Companion Dog Excellent). We were progressing nicely until he started refusing to jump the relatively low jumps required for a dog of his small size. Even though this was before I had crossed over to force-free training, I was smart enough to not punish him for his 'disobedience' but instead realized that we needed to see if there was a medical issue. Sure enough, my little eight-pound boy had hip dysplasia (go figure!) and it was hurting him to jump. We retired from the obedience ring and shared happy times doing other things together for his remaining years.

Once you have confirmed that your dog *doesn't* have a medical problem, you can try to gain her willing consent for the activities you would like her to enjoy. If your dog loves running in the woods, set up an agility jump (or several) on the hiking trail and let her hop over them on your hike. Incorporate other play activities with an occasional dance move or dash through a tunnel—play tug, toss a ball, do a quick dance move and toss the ball again. Do her favorite tricks, run through a tunnel and do more tricks.

Evaluate the environment where she is declining to play. If she does all her agility equipment happily at home, but clearly isn't enjoying classes or competitions, what's different about those places that she's not happy about? Is it the chaos of all the other dogs around? The loudspeaker at competition venues? Or maybe your own stress in those places? If you can identify what's bothering her, you may be able to condition her to enjoy those locations as well.

But be careful! If you try to do too much too soon you can **poison** the beloved activity (give it a negative association) and your dog could end up disliking that activity as well. She may refuse to jump over those jumps in the woods, stop playing tug, and quit chasing the ball that she used to love so much. Go slow and remember to keep it fun and light. Our dogs often become worried when we seem tense and worried, especially when we are nervous or very intense about competition. Keep it fun—and keep doing those consent tests. If you can get your dog to love it and happily consent to the activity, you're good to go.

### Other consent options

Another option may be to find a different activity that your dog *does* enjoy. If Agility wasn't her thing, maybe she'll go for Musical

Freestyle (dancing with your dog), or Treibball (herding large, inflated balls into nets—check out the National Association of Treibball Enthusiasts) or Rally (a more fun, relaxed version of "obedience" competition), or Scent Work (lots of dogs love to be encouraged to use their noses). A friend of mine started an organization called Missing Animal Response Network—they train dogs to find missing pets. Now wouldn't *that* be a fun and rewarding thing to do!

Your other choice? Get another dog. Seriously. Keep the first one of course, but if you have your heart set on doing therapy, agility or some other activity and your current dog is telling you she hates it, your best option may be to adopt another dog who has great potential for that. Do some consent testing first to be sure she isn't going to tell you "No thanks" from the start and then go for it. And for your first dog—take some time to find out what *she* wants to do and then do that with her.

**THE CHOICE TO CHOOSE**

BEHAVIOUR PROBLEMS ARE LESS LIKELY WHEN DOGS ARE GIVEN AN APPROPRIATE CHOICE

THE USE OF FORCE / FEAR / PUNISHMENT / PHYSICAL MANIPULATION REMOVES CHOICE / HAS NEGATIVE CONSEQUENCES

**BENEFITS OF CHOICE**

- Builds self confidence & trust
- Decreases fear / stress / anxiety
- Builds problem solving skills
- Increases resilience
- Creates a sense of security
- Prevents learned helplessness
- Improves well being
- Improves quality of life
- Correct choices can be rewarded
- We see what motivates behaviour

**WAYS TO PROVIDE CHOICE**

- To disengage / walk away
- To interact with a person / dog
- To consent to touch
- Move closer without luring
- Take a break / stop an activity
- Sniff / explore when out walking
- Choose which direction to walk
- Which area to rest or sleep
- Which toy / game to play
- Choice of different treats / food

We control just about every aspect of our dogs' lives - allowing simple choices provides so many benefits

Dogs Disclosed

# Chapter 11

## Nose Brain Candy Games: I Sniff, Therefore I Am

---

**Key cognitive processes for improving and enhancing training:**

- **Perceiving**
- **Volition**
- **Discrimination**

Now that we know dogs can self-identify through their olfactory abilities—a cognitive skill—we realize that their amazing sense of smell can also be put to good use through other cognitive talents. We have long utilized our dogs' incredible sense of smell to identify contraband, help save endangered wildlife, recover lost possessions, locate missing persons and find missing pets. Yes, this is a cognitive behavior—the dog must grasp the concept that she is to look for the thing—or the scent—that you are asking her to look for. That's actually a sophisticated cognitive concept that we've been using with our dogs for a very long time—long before we accepted that they were cognitive!

Sources don't seem to agree on the power of the dog's nose compared to a human. Sciencenews.org estimates range from anywhere from 1,000 to 100,000 to even a million times stronger than the human sense of smell. We humans are estimated to have around five million sensory receptors in our noses, where dogs may have as many as 100 million to 300 million or more, depending on your source for information. Plus, the area of the brain that analyzes odors is also about forty times larger in dogs than in humans, giving them an additional olfactory processing advantage.

However, we shouldn't sell our human noses too short. One of the more reliable sources for canine nose information is Dr. Nathanial Hall, Director of the Canine Olfaction Research and Education Laboratory at Texas Tech University. I was quite impressed by Dr. Hall several years ago when he spoke at the annual Pet Professional Guild conference about canine olfaction.

"You might not realize," he said, "how good your own noses really are. Next time you see your dog sniffing something, get down on your hands and knees and smell the same spot yourself. You will likely be quite surprised by how much you are able to smell!" Then he added with a smile, "Just don't let your clients see you doing it."

*The amazing canine nose.*

## Specific Scent Detection

There are two different types of scent work that we use with our dogs—"Specific Scent Detection" and "Smell This Smell, Find This Smell." They both have valuable but different applications.

**Specific Scent Detection** work dogs are taught to look for one or more specific odors and *only* those odors. This type of scent work has a very long list of useful applications, including but by no means limited to training for narcotics, explosives and arson detection, cadaver location, endangered species preservation, identification of illegal agricultural product importation at airports and borders, and the detection of a long list of other unlawful activities or undesirable species. These dogs generally work with police departments or other government agencies. Specific Scent Detection is also used commercially for bedbugs and other pest detection and for a variety of medical purposes including diabetic and seizure alert and cancer detection. Very useful indeed!

It is also used when training dogs for the competitive sports of K9 Nosework and in Tracking competitions. Drug detection dogs might be taught to only look for cocaine, fentanyl, heroin, methamphetamine or more. Arson detection dogs look for the scent of gasoline and other odors related to fire-setting. Conservation dogs look for the scat (feces) of whatever species they are working to help in their environment. Cadaver dogs are, obviously, trained to track down the scent of dead bodies. Because these various applications of scent work employ different types of training, you would do well to find a qualified trainer in your area who specializes in the type of scent detection work that you would like to do.

## Smell This Smell, Find This Smell

This variation of scent detection is somewhat simpler and something you can just have fun with at home with your own dog. Of course, it also has a variety of very useful applications—it is the kind of scent work used with missing persons, lost pets and in Tracking competitions, where a human lays a track by walking, usually in a field, and the dog must follow that track to find the person, animal or an object.

There are various Search and Rescue organizations you can work with if you want to engage in finding missing persons.

Again, if you want to take a serious dive into this type of work, I encourage you to contact a credentialed, qualified trainer. However, if you just want to engage your dog with some unbelievable fun (and brain tiring) cognitive scent work in the comfort of your own home, you can try the nose games listed below which are good for almost any dog and human.

## Nose Games played inside

I suggest that you start this in the comfort of your own home where there are few distractions. After your dog is rocking it, feel free to take it on the road!

Nose games involve teaching your dog to look for and find hidden objects when you ask him to. This is an exceptionally useful game as it uses lots of energy and can tire out your very active dog, plus it has very practical applications as well. We start with treats since most dogs will happily look for food. You can eventually ask him to look for hidden objects (favorite toys, your lost keys) and even hidden or missing humans!

As you are working your way through the steps below you will also want to teach your dog a "Mark" behavior (in separate training sessions) so that when the treat, object, pet or human they are seeking is in a location where they cannot reach it, they have a way to let you know. As soon as you start hiding treats where your dog can't get to them you can start asking her for the "Mark" behavior. (See Teaching the Mark below.)

Here's how to start with Nose Games:

**Step 1:**

1. Have your dog sit and stay. (If she doesn't know sit/stay, have someone hold her leash.)
2. Walk six feet away, show her a treat, remind her to stay (you can repeat "Wait" or "Stay" as often as necessary) and place

the treat on the ground. If the floor is a dark color, a light-colored treat will be easier for her to find—she will be using her vision at first—and vice versa if the floor is light colored.

3. Return to her side, remind her to "Stay!" You don't want her to get up yet! Turn and face the treat, then tell her, "Search!"—or whatever cue you want to use. (If she won't get up until you release her from the stay, say "Search!" and then give your release cue.) She should run right out and eat the treat.
4. **Important note: Do NOT point to the treat. We want her to look for it on her own, we do not want her to learn to wait for you to show her where it is. If she's having trouble at any time during the search you can indicate an area by spreading your arms wide in the general vicinity of the treat, but do not point to it.**
5. Repeat a half-dozen times varying the length of time you wait each time before you release her. You don't want her to think that you returning to her is the release.

**Step 2:**

1. Have your dog sit and stay.
2. Let her watch you hide a treat in plain view on the ground but in a slightly more difficult location (next to a chair leg, by a waste basket, etc.).
3. Return to her side (reminder her to stay!), turn and face the treat, then tell her to "Search!" (Release if necessary.) She should run right out and eat the treat.
4. Repeat a half-dozen times remembering to vary the length of time you wait before sending her to search.

**Step 3:**

1. Have your dog sit and stay.
2. Let her watch you hide *several* treats in plain view on the ground.
3. Return to her side (don't let her get up!), turn and face the treats, rub one of the treats you're using on a paper towel,

hold the towel in front of her nose (don't let her eat it!) and tell her, "Sniff!" Don't worry if she doesn't appear to sniff it, her nose is plenty good enough to catch the scent even if she doesn't appear to take a deep breath. This step is the beginning of the actual "smell this smell, find this smell" piece.

4. Then tell her, "Search!" She should run right out and eat the treats.
5. Repeat a half-dozen times, having her "Sniff" before each set of multiple treats.

**Remember do NOT point to the treat. If she's having trouble, indicate an area. If she's really having trouble, you may have made it too hard too soon. Reset, pick up the treat(s) that she couldn't find and do another round with easier hides this time.**

**Step 4:**

1. Have your dog sit and stay.
2. Let her watch you hide one treat in a harder place (behind a chair leg, etc.).
3. Return to her side (don't let her get up!), turn and face the treat, cue her to "Sniff!," and then cue her to, "Search!" She may have more difficulty finding this treat. Don't help her other than to indicate a broad area, if she needs it. If she truly can't find it, reset, and hide it in an easier spot. Make sure she watches you!
4. Repeat a half-dozen times.
5. Gradually hide the treat in harder places, still on the ground, having her "Sniff" before each set.

*Start hiding in harder places.*

**Step 5:**

1. Have your dog sit and stay.
2. Let her watch you hide two or three treats in somewhat easy places (behind a chair leg, etc.).
3. Return to her side (don't let her get up!), turn and face the treats, then tell her, "Search!" She may have more difficulty finding multiple treats. If necessary, indicate an area by spreading your arms and saying, "Search here!" Don't point to the treat! This is where she starts learning to use her nose. If you help her, she won't learn to use her nose, she'll learn to wait for you to help her. If she truly can't find it, reset and hide it in a slightly easier spot. Make sure she is watching you!
4. Repeat a half-dozen times.
5. Gradually hide treats in harder spots, giving the "Sniff" cue and having her "Sniff" again each time before you send her. Begin hiding on raised surfaces—these are even harder for her to find because the scent moves in different patterns with air currents as it drifts down toward the ground.

*Raised surfaces are even harder.*

**Step 6:**

Now it gets *really* challenging!

1. Put your dog in another room.
2. Hide 2 to 3 treats in somewhat easy places.
3. Bring her back to the room, have her "Sniff!" then tell her "Search!" She may have more difficulty finding multiple treats. If necessary, indicate an area by spreading your arms and saying, "Search here!" Don't point to the treat! If you help her, she won't use her nose, she'll wait for you to show her. If she truly can't find it, reset and hide it in a slightly easier spot.
4. Repeat a half-dozen times, doing "Sniff" each time.
5. Gradually hide treats in harder spots.

**Step 7:**

1. Generalize your dog's search behavior to other scents at first, then other objects as you desire, starting with a favorite toy. Rub the toy on the paper towel and start back at Step 1 placing the toy in plain view, then moving quickly through to Step 6.
2. Then use less favorite or neutral objects. For humans, rub the human's scent on the paper towel by having them rub it on their neck or armpit, and then have them hide in easy places at first. Let the dog find them in plain view, then watch them hide behind a barrier or around a corner, then all the way through Step 6.

## Teaching the mark behavior

To teach your dog a mark behavior, you can use something she already knows and just teach her to offer it when she makes a find, using a new cue specific to that situation, or you can teach her an entirely new behavior. Typical behaviors include lying down, sitting and barking. I teach my dog to mark by using a simple cue like "Down." Many dogs already know a down behavior and it's easy to transfer it to this new situation as their find indicator cue. (Note that there may be specific techniques to teach a mark for various scent activities—ask your trainer!)

Here's how:

- Choose your verbal mark cue. I use "Mark!"
- Say "Mark," pause for two to four seconds, then cue and/or prompt your Mark behavior. "Mark!" Pause. "Down!"
- After a few repetitions (the number can vary widely from one dog to the next) you will see your dog lie down after you say, "Mark" before you have a chance to say, "Down!" Keep practicing this until she consistently lies down on your "Mark!" cue.

Now you're ready to integrate it into your Nose Games:

- Hide a treat where your dog can't access it without your help.
- Give her a "Sniff!" of the scented paper towel and tell her to "Search!"
- Follow her to where the treat is and when you can tell that she's trying to get to it tell her to "Mark!" and then give your "Down!" cue if necessary.
- Take out the treat and give it to her. If your hidden object is a toy, take it out and play with it with her. If it's something not edible or playable, use your clicker or other reward marker and then feed her a treat or play with a toy from your pocket.
- Repeat until she will lie down on just the "Mark!" cue without you having to say "Down!"
- Then repeat until she starts to offer her Mark behavior when she finds the hidden treat or object on her own without you having to give the "Mark!" cue.
- Continue to repeat until she consistently offers her Mark behavior without you having to give the cue. CONGRATULATIONS!!!

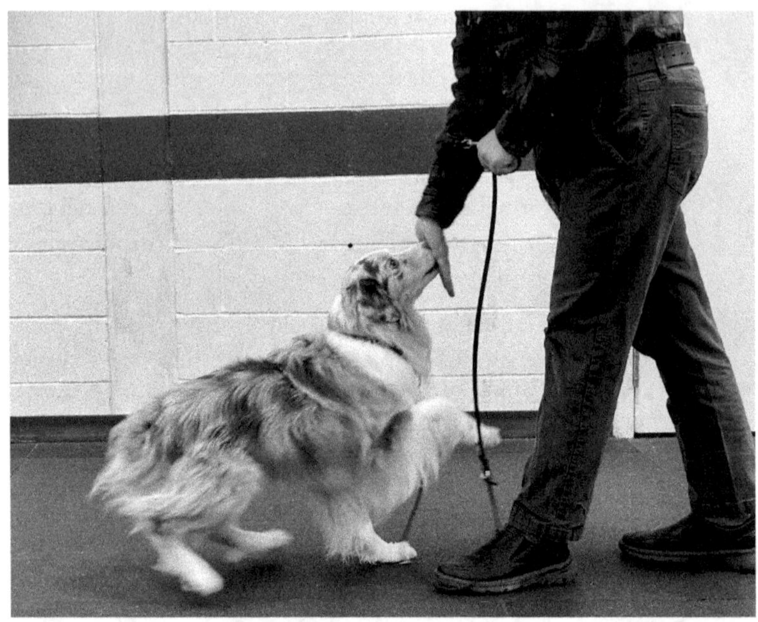

*Teaching the Mark with a nose touch.*

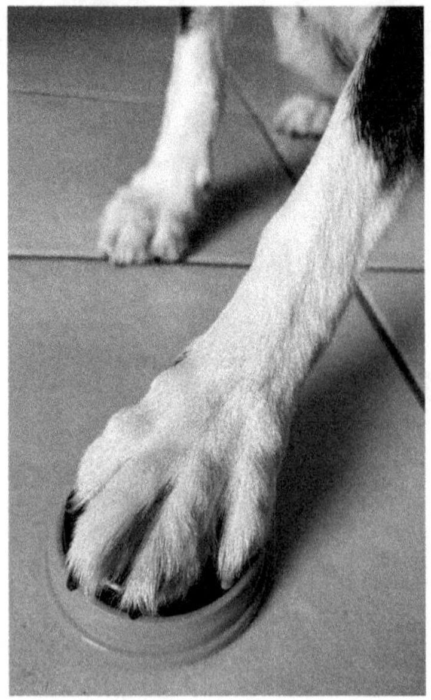

*Teaching the Mark with a paw touch.*

## Taking it on the road

Now you're ready to take it on the road! When your dog is solid on the seven Nose Games steps and consistently marks the treats or objects she can't get to without being cued, try doing Nose Games elsewhere. Outdoors at first, in the comfort of your own backyard (if you have one), then in more and more foreign locations. Start again with Step 1, setting her up to succeed. You should be able to quickly move through to Step 7 in each new location.

I have at times offered a six-week Nose Games class to my students. They loved it. Not only is it fun for dog and human alike, but because scent work is very brain-tiring for the dog it is great mental enrichment and tires your dog out without having to take her for a 10-mile hike or play Frisbee in the back yard for a half-hour.

I had a student who took the six-week class twice with her small Terrier mix dog and her eight-year-old son. By the end of the second six weeks Ricky could go hide in the woods and Checkers could find him in short order. Pretty impressive!

Here is my Nose Games class curriculum:

### Week 1

- Discussion of scent work
- Reading your dog
- Find It Toss—treats
- Find It in Plain View—treats
- Find It Hidden in Plain View—treats
- Cues

### Week 2

- Review
- Take Scent
- Work with Toys/Objects
- Hidden in Same Room—treats and objects
- Outside Work

**Week 3**

- Review
- Hidden in Box
- Push/Mark

**Week 4**

- Review
- New Rooms
- Where?
- Check This

**Week 5**

- Review

**Week 6**

- Graduation—Find owner

# Chapter 12

# Reading, Writing and 'Rithmatic—and Painting

## More Challenging Brain Candy Games

---

**Key cognitive processes for improving and enhancing training:**

- **Perceiving**
- **Recognizing**
- **Volition**
- **Conceiving**
- **Problem Solving**
- **Reasoning**
- **Memory**
- **Learning**

### Who Knew …?

Do you know that dogs can read? Count? And even write? I know, I didn't believe it either until I saw videos and decided to try it for myself. It is nothing short of incredible, and I'm betting that once you know how you'll be crazy-eager to try it with your dog.

The following three games require that your dog can understand and apply these concepts:

1. Black squiggles on a white board have meaning.
2. Quantity is a "thing."
3. Your dog can make black squiggles that also have meaning.

Of the three, I believe that reading is the easiest (believe it or not!) so we'll start with that one.

## Reading

Dr. Bonnie Bergin founded Canine Companions for Independence more than 30 years ago. The dogs she worked with were so intelligent and responsive that from time to time she thought about teaching them to read. The idea stayed in the back of her mind until 2002, when she began a canine reading experiment, and then wrote a book, along with co-author Sharon Hogan, which was published in 2006 with the intriguing title of *Teach Your Dog to Read.*

When I first heard about dogs reading, I thought, "Well, that's just looking at black squiggles on paper and … Wait!!! That's what reading is!!!" So, we incorporated reading into our cognition teachings with great success. Here's how you can teach your dog to read:

1. Make two white signs that are identical in size and shape, with the word SIT in large black letters on one sign and the word DOWN on the other.
2. With your dog standing in front of you, hold up the SIT sign, pause, then verbally cue your dog to sit. When your dog sits, mark with your clicker or verbal marker and feed him a treat. Lure or prompt if necessary. (If your dog won't stay in a standing position, see the Helping Your Dog Stand section below.)
3. Repeat Step 2 until you can hold up the sign and your dog sits without you having to say, "Sit," with no luring or prompting. He now thinks holding up a white square with black squiggles on it is a new cue for "Sit."

*Teaching to read SIT.*

4. Now hold up the DOWN sign in the exact same position you previously held up the SIT sign, pause, and verbally cue your dog to down. Lure or prompt if necessary. When he lies down, mark and treat.

5. Repeat Step 4 until you can hold up the sign and your dog lies down without you having to say, "Down" and with no luring or prompting. He now thinks you've changed your mind and that holding up a white square with black squiggles is the new cue for "Down."

*Teaching to read DOWN.*

6. Now randomly vary which sign you hold up in the exact same position. Pause and cue the appropriate behavior until you see that your dog is beginning to offer the correct behavior in response to whichever sign you hold up. If you realize he's about to make a mistake (i.e., he starts to lie down when you hold up the SIT sign) cheerfully help him get it right—verbally cue the "Sit" and lure him back up into position.
7. Continue to repeat Step 6 until your dog is offering the correct behavior 80% or more of the time. He is now recognizing that one set of squiggles means he should sit and the other means he should lie down. He can interpret the meaning of the squiggles and offer the correct behavior—that's reading!
8. If you want to take it further, make additional cue cards for behaviors your dog knows and use the same procedure to teach him new words. Note that if you use cues that require

a body prompt from you, you won't really know if he's reading the card or responding to your prompt (i.e., shake—where you offer your hand; touch—where he touches his nose to your offered fist), so it's best to stick to behaviors where you don't have to move to invite a response.

Here are some other options (of course these are all behaviors you would need to teach him *before* trying to teach him to read the words):

- **Paw**: Lifting his paw or touching his foot to something stationary on the floor or a stool.
- **Spin**: Doing a counterclockwise turn, and/or twirl—a clockwise turn.
- **Bravo**: Taking a bow—lowering his front end while keeping his hindquarters elevated.
- **Boing**: Leaping straight up in the air off all four feet.
- **Sit Pretty**: Sitting flat on his hind end while lifting his front paws up in a begging position.
- **Mat** (or **Place**, or **Bed**): Going to his designated mat and lying down on it.

You get the idea, there are many behaviors you can teach your dog to associate with black squiggles and learn to perform the designated behavior by reading the squiggles.

### Reading sentences

Want to go one step beyond and really wow your friends? Let's try teaching your dog to read sentences! In English, we read from left to right so let's do it that way, teaching your dog to read from *his* left to right.

Since a lot of dogs will start to offer an auto-down from a sit, I suggest using different behaviors than you have taught your dog to read for your first attempt at teaching a sentence, or at least not in Sit/Down order. Let's say you taught your dog to spin. Your sentence might be: "Spin, Down, Sit."

1. You'll start with two words—"Spin" and "Down"—or whatever two words will work best for your genius dog. With

your dog standing in front of you, hold up your "Spin" sign in your right hand. (See "Helping your dog stand" below for tips if needed.)

2. As soon as your dog spins, pause, keep your SPIN sign in place, then hold up your DOWN sign in your left hand a foot to the side from your SPIN card. Since reading two signs in a row is new to him, you might have to cue the second behavior.

3. When your dog can read the two behaviors in a row with a pause in between without any cues, gradually decrease the pause until there is barely any delay between spin and down behaviors. Continue to cue as needed.

4. Next, slowly decrease the distance between the cards until they are right next to each other, still with only a slight pause between them and with your dog still doing the two behaviors in a row correctly.

5. Now hold up both cards in your right hand at the same time so they read: SPIN DOWN from your right-to-left (from your dog's left-to-right). Cue as needed.

6. Your next step is to add your third card—again another behavior that your dog reads easily. Repeat steps 3 through 6, this time with your first two cards in your right hand, and your new, third card in your left hand. Perhaps it now looks like: SPIN DOWN SIT.

7. Continue this until your dog can read three cards in a row. Now you can add more cards if you want and perhaps try mixing them up in a different order to see if he's really reading—or if perhaps he's just learned a behavior chain.

Just remember that our dogs are capable of far more amazing feats of cognition than we've given them credit for in the past. When your dog is reading sentences, I want you to let me know!

**Helping your dog stand**
Your dog needs to start in the standing position for each of your reading cards. You should make the effort to teach your dog a solid stand behavior which is what he will be doing when he is not 'reading.' Here are four easy hacks to teach reading without cueing the stand behavior:

1. Step backwards and invite your dog to follow you. As he does, hold up your SIT card, then stop moving, pause, and give your verbal, "Sit" cue (then prompt or lure if needed).
2. Stand still and toss a treat away from you so your dog moves away to get it. As he moves back toward you, hold up your SIT card, pause, and give your verbal "Sit" cue (then prompt or lure if needed).
3. Cue your dog to "Wait" or "Stay" while you back eight to ten feet away from him, then invite him to you. When he gets close to you, hold up your SIT card, pause, and give your verbal "Sit" cue (then prompt or lure if needed).
4. Do the same thing as needed with your DOWN card and any of your other reading cards.

## Counting

So now … how about counting? We were once told that dogs could maybe count to three, but the amazing Ken Ramirez, Executive Vice-President and Chief Training Officer of Karen Pryor Clicker Training, has proven that dogs are capable of far more than that in his book *The Eye of the Trainer*. Ken did his research at Chicago's Shedd Aquarium where he developed and supervised animal care, animal health programs, staff training and development as well as public presentation programs for the entire animal collection of more than 32,000 animals. He worked at Shedd for nearly 26 years and has been a leader in educating the professional dog behavior and training world about science-based training. So when Ken suggested—and demonstrated—that dogs could count beyond three, people listened.

He started by teaching his canine student to associate a number of objects (1, 2, or 3) with shapes. A blue circle was one, a green rectangle was two, and a black triangle was three. Lest you think we're still hung up on brilliant Border Collies, his willing protégée was a three-year-old rescued Airedale Terrier mix named Coral.

With input from other behavior scientists, Ken next began asking Coral to associate the number of objects in a tray with magnetic dots on a whiteboard. This meant she had to count twice—first counting the number of objects in the tray, then the number of dots on the board. Using this method, she was able to count from one to five with 95% accuracy and six to eight with 90% accuracy. Very impressive and well above chance!

Finally, Ken added Match to Sample (See Chapter 9.) to Coral's counting prowess. He put a number of different objects in the tray and held up the object that he wanted her to count. There might be six red Kongs, two yellow tennis balls, three green plastic rings, three blue discs, etc. If he held up a yellow tennis ball, she counted the balls in the tray and touched the board that had two dots. If he held up a red Kong, she counted the Kongs in the tray and touched the board that had six dots. Coral was able to achieve a remarkable accuracy rating of 79% for up to 14 items—still well above chance.

So now that Ken has provided us with plenty of evidence that dogs can in fact be taught to count, want to give it a try? Here's how:

1. Gather several similar objects—a half-dozen balls, Kongs, plastic rings or cups, for example. Obtain several magnetic whiteboards and a number of magnetic dots that will stick to it (you can Google these).
2. Put one dot on a board and lean it against a wall or chair so your dog can easily see it.
3. Place one object in a tray, draw your dog's attention to it and ask, "How many?"
4. Encourage her to nose touch or paw touch the dot on the board. Mark and treat.
5. Repeat until she will touch the dot on the board when asked, "How many?" without you having to prompt her. Mark and treat each time.

6. Now place a second board next to the first one with two dots on it. Place two items in the tray, draw her attention to it, and ask, "How many?" If she touches the "one" dot, just don't say anything, and wait to see if she then tries touching the board with two dots. If she does, mark and treat. If she doesn't, you can draw her attention to the board with two dots and mark and treat when she touches it.
7. Repeat with both target boards, sometimes with one object in the tray, sometimes with two objects, helping her succeed until she can consistently get it right. This will take some time—be patient!
8. Add a third item to the tray and a board with three dots, repeat the above steps until she can successfully count to three. Over time, you can increase the number even more until you get to what you find is your dog's optimum number to count.
9. If you want to get even more complex, add Ken's "Match to Sample" element.

*Teaching to Count.*

A 2019 study conducted at Emory University in Atlanta, Georgia by Lauren Aulet et al, supports a conclusion that that dogs do have the ability to count even without special training.

Just so you know, as much as we are excited about our dogs' ability to count—we have yet to see any evidence that they are capable of adding, subtracting, doing long division, multiplication, fractions, algebra or calculus. But you never know. …

## Writing

Writing is by far the most challenging of the three behaviors introduced in this chapter. In fact, I've only seen it once, done by the wonderful Emily Larlham of Kikopup and Dogmantics at a dog trainer conference. I watched as one of Emily's dogs took and held a marker in his mouth and wrote an actual word on a whiteboard. I will admit it knocked my socks off—and I confess I have yet to try it with my own dogs.

Emily had taught her dog to hold the marker and move it from one dot to the next—and then she put dots on the board to guide her dog's writing into an actual word. I could be wrong, but as far as I could tell the dog didn't know the meaning of the word he was writing. Still, it was pretty impressive—and if you combined it with the reading protocol from the previous section, I'm willing to bet you could eventually end up with a dog who did know—and could read—the word(s) he was writing.

So go ahead, knock my socks off again. Be sure to let me know when your dog is writing sentences and then performing the behaviors he has written in the sentence. Can't wait to hear from you!

## Painting

Wait a minute … Painting? Is that truly cognitive? For humans it definitely is—I don't honestly know if it is for dogs or not—but maybe it could be. We did Painting in an Advanced Cognition Academy—and while you could teach a dog to hold a brush in his mouth and paint, our students all had their dogs put their paws in the paint and create art that way. They did come up with some stunning pieces … but I think you'd have to do a lot more than we did to determine if dogs can really make artistic decisions about what they want to paint and appreciate the results. But, just like the other cognitive talents we didn't think dogs were capable of in the past, it wouldn't surprise me if someday a relative of Chaser started painting masterpieces!

*Dogs can Paint! The setup.*

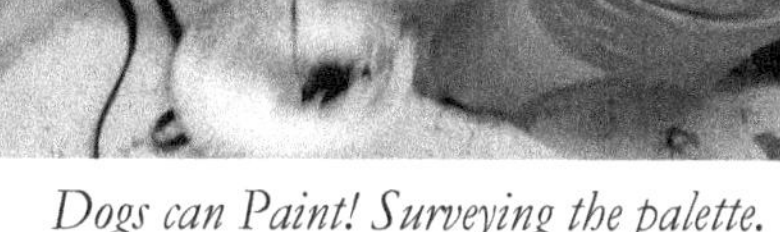

*Dogs can Paint! Surveying the palette.*

*Dogs can Paint! The finished product.*

# Chapter 13

## Copy That

### Dogs Can't Imitate …
### Or Maybe They Can!

---

**Key cognitive processes for improving and enhancing training:**

- **Perceiving**
- **Recognizing**
- **Volition**
- **Conceiving**
- **Imitation**
- **Problem Solving**
- **Reasoning**
- **Memory**
- **Anticipating**
- **Learning**

## One more cognitive door opens

I remember, years ago, confidently and assertively telling my training academy students, "Dogs don't learn through imitation." That's what behavior scientists were telling us, but over time the scientists were proven wrong (as was I). That's a great thing, because the studies that have now clearly established this ability in dogs are incredibly exciting. Their findings have expanded our ability to train and communicate with our dogs, and imitation protocols are now being used by legions of dog lovers.

First, there was a study in the early 1990's in which a litter of puppies was placed in a pen and could access the handle of a wagon that had food in it—food that the puppies wanted to eat. A second litter of puppies was allowed to watch the first litter engaging in this task. The researchers timed the first litter to see how long it took them to figure out how to pull the wagon into the pen and then allowed the second litter to try it. They repeated this with multiple litters and when they looked at their data, they found that it took the first litter an average of 20 minutes to pull the wagon into the pen and the second litter an average of 5 minutes. Clearly those puppies were learning something by watching and then imitating the behaviors of the first litter when given the opportunity to access the food for themselves.

Then, there was a 1997 study in which puppies were allowed to watch their narcotics detection dog mothers while working in a real-life work environment. When the pups were six months old, the ones who watched their mothers at work learned the tasks more easily and quickly than puppies who had not been allowed to watch their mothers at work. Again, clearly, they were learning something that they were able to implement, i.e., imitate, when put to the task.

"Okay," we were told, "so puppies can learn through imitation by watching other dogs." It makes good biological survival sense that the young of a species can learn by watching others. If they had to learn everything from scratch all on their own, they would be far less likely to survive. "But," we were cautioned, "adult dogs certainly *cannot* learn through imitation."

But then Ken Ramirez (Yes, the same Ken Ramirez from Chicago's world-famous Shedd Aquarium who taught his dog to count.) taught his dog that the cue, "Copy!" means "Do what that other dog just did." When he shared his "Copy!" procedure at Karen Pryor's Clicker Expo in 2011, the dog training world sat up and took notice. "Okay, cool!," we said, "Dogs *can* learn by imitating other dogs! "But," we were still warned by the behavior science community, "they certainly cannot imitate *humans*!"

Then, only two years later, Italian PhD ethologist Claudia Fugazza, who was studying at Eotvos Lorand University in Budapest, conducting research on social learning and imitation with Professor Adam Miklosi, said, "Wanna bet???!!!" Claudia developed a training method she calls "Do As I Do," which relies on a dog's social cognitive skills to learn new behaviors by imitating humans. Did you get that? Claudia showed us in no uncertain terms that dogs can learn new behaviors by imitating human behavior. The second edition of Claudia's book *Do As I Do* was just published by Dogwise last year.

Skeptic that I am, I ordered the DVD and was completely and totally gobsmacked. (You can access the video on demand from Dogwise.com.). I was so taken by the procedure I immediately decided to try it with Bonnie, my eight-year-old Scorgidoodle.

## A little prep work

It was a humbling experience. For starters, your dog has to know at least three behaviors (other than "Sit!") on verbal cue—without any body prompting, gestures or even a sideways shift of the eyes. This is necessary in order to avoid inadvertently giving him a very subtle cue to perform (see The Clever Hans Phenomenon below).

Note that the behaviors all have to be things you can demonstrate to your dog yourself—you cannot, for example, crawl through your own legs. Your demonstration should be as close as possible to how you want your dog to do the behavior. If you want her to sit on a stool you should sit on the stool. If you want her to lie down on a blanket you should lie down on the blanket. However, you *can* use what's called **functional imitation**—dogs know we pick things up with our hands and they can't pick them up with their paws, so if we pick something up with our hand, they will know to pick it up with their mouths.

Be sure to practice your demonstration behaviors without your dog present at first so you become very adept at them before asking your dog to copy you. Then you can begin.

For my dog Bonnie, I selected the behaviors Down, Tap (touch an Easy Button with a paw), and Up (step up and sit on a "Stepper"). I discovered that Bonnie's Down behavior was solidly on verbal cue, but we needed some work on Tap and Up to fade my very natural, subtle but unacceptable body prompts. After several brush-up sessions focusing on those two verbal cues, we were ready to proceed. If you want to see how clean your verbal cues, video yourself working with your dog to see how much brushing up you might need to do prior to jumping into imitation work.

**The Clever Hans story**

Clever Hans was a German Orlav Trotter Horse stallion in the early 1900s who made headlines by allegedly solving math problems and perform other amazing tasks. According to his owner, math teacher, amateur horse trainer and mystic Wilhelm von Osten, Hans could add, subtract, multiply, divide, work with fractions, tell time, keep track of the calendar, differentiate musical tones, and read, spell and understand German. When given a math problem orally or in writing Hans would answer correctly by tapping his hoof.

Von Osten's clever horse drew so much public attention that a commission was appointed by the German Board of Education to investigate his outlandish claims. The Hans Commission consisted of thirteen people including a veterinarian, a circus manager, a Cavalry officer, a number of schoolteachers and the Director of the Berlin Zoological Gardens. After extensive examination, in September 1904, the commission determined that no tricks were involved in Hans's performance, that he really appeared to perform the incredible feats that von Osten claimed.

Still not convinced, the commission recruited Oskar Pfungst, a German comparative biologist and psychologist, to explore the claims further. Pfungst found that Hans could get the correct answer even if von Osten himself did not ask the questions, ruling out the possibility of intentional fraud. However, Hans got the right answer only when the questioner knew what the answer was and only if the horse could see the questioner. Pfungst determined that when Von Osten knew the answers to the questions Hans got 89% of the answers correct, but when Von Osten did not know the answers to the questions his correct answer score plummeted to six percent.

Pfungst then studied the behavior of the questioner and determined that as Hans's taps approached the right answer, the questioner's posture and facial expression showed an increase in tension, then relaxed when the horse made the final, correct tap. The questioner's body language was clearly, albeit unintentionally, providing a cue that prompted Hans to stop tapping. Pfungst believed that Van Osten really thought Hans was answering the questions and was not deliberately perpetrating a fraud.

Based on the research of Oskar Pfungst and a second investigator, Ernst Timaeus, eight sources of cueing by Von Osten and others working with the horse have been identified:

1. Eyes: blinking, changes in direction.
2. Head: head movements upwards, downwards and sideways.
3. Mouth: changes in lip configuration.
4. Body: changes in postural tension.
5. Hands: hand movements.
6. Jaw: changes in muscle tension.
7. Voiceless counting along.
8. Breathing: patterns of inhalation.

Today when an animal appears to be brilliant and is suspected of responding to the handler's unintentional cues, the Clever Hans phenomenon is suspected unless and until proved otherwise. Thanks to Clever Hans, protocols such as the "double-blind study" were developed to prevent subjects from responding to cues given inadvertently by the researchers.

Clever Hans may not really have been doing math, but it was certainly very clever of him to figure out how to read human body language well enough to answer the questions correctly and, undoubtedly, be reinforced for it. Your dog is undoubtedly as clever as Clever Hans so if you're teaching your dog to Copy That, be sure you're not giving any inadvertent body language cues!

## How can dogs learn to imitate

### Imitation: Phase 1

Phase 1 involves teaching your dog the imitation concept. That is, whatever behavior you do followed by the cue "Copy!" means "You are supposed to do the same behavior." I chose to use "Copy!" rather than Fugazza's suggested cue of "Do it!" because I use that cue in other training games I play with my dogs. A clever trainer-friend of mine uses "Xerox!" You can, of course, use whatever cue you'd like, if it's not the same as or similar to any other cues you use.

**Here's what Phase 1 looks like:**

1. Stand facing your dog, three to six feet away from her. Claudia originally said six feet. We have since found that some dogs aren't accustomed to performing behaviors at a six-foot distance from their human and that it *can* work if you are closer—although it's better if you can do the six feet. You can mark your starting position, and your dog's, with tape on the floor to help you make sure you're both starting in the same place every time.
2. Note that your dog must always be in the same starting position. If you use a different starting position for different behaviors, you are giving your dog a huge Clever Hans tip off for which behavior you are about to demonstrate. I use Stand for my dogs' starting position.
3. If you are using props, put *all* your props out before you start. If you stop in the middle to put a prop in place you are giving your dog a *big* clue that you are about to use that prop next. Clever Hans!
4. Tell your dog, "Wait" or "Stay," and then, "Watch." I like to tell my dog "Watch" before demonstrating and point my index finger at the corner of my eye as both a verbal and visual cue to get her attention and let her know I am about to demonstrate the behavior I want her to copy.
5. Demonstrate your first behavior. Perhaps it's a Down. Turn sideways to your dog so she can see you better and lie down

using as close an approximation as possible to the way a dog lies down.

6. Return to your starting position and stand with your arms relaxed at your side.
7. Say, "Copy," give your release cue if your dog needs permission to be released from her "Wait" or "Stay" cue, pause for three seconds, and then give your verbal cue, "Down!" with no Clever Hansing! If necessary, give a prompt after your verbal cue. (We have learned, since Claudia introduced "Do As I Do" in 2013, that dogs can learn to imitate if their behaviors are not as solidly on verbal cue as we would like—but it's not ideal, it's harder and it takes longer).
8. You can repeat your first behavior *three times and only three times*—then you must move on to your second behavior. If you repeat the same behavior too many times in a row your dog will think, "Copy" is just a new cue for "Down." We need the dog to understand that it's a *concept* that means "Do whatever I just did," and it can cue a variety of behaviors.
9. Now repeat Steps 4-9 with your second behavior and then with your third.

It is important to pause for a few seconds each time after you say "Copy," so your dog's brain has time to process the cue. Eventually, you will say, "Copy" and during your pause your dog will do the behavior you just demonstrated. CELEBRATE! Your dog is starting to understand the concept! Continue to practice until she can consistently succeed in copying your behavior without the verbal cue at least 80% of the time. Congratulations, you're ready for Phase 2!

*Imitation Demonstration.*

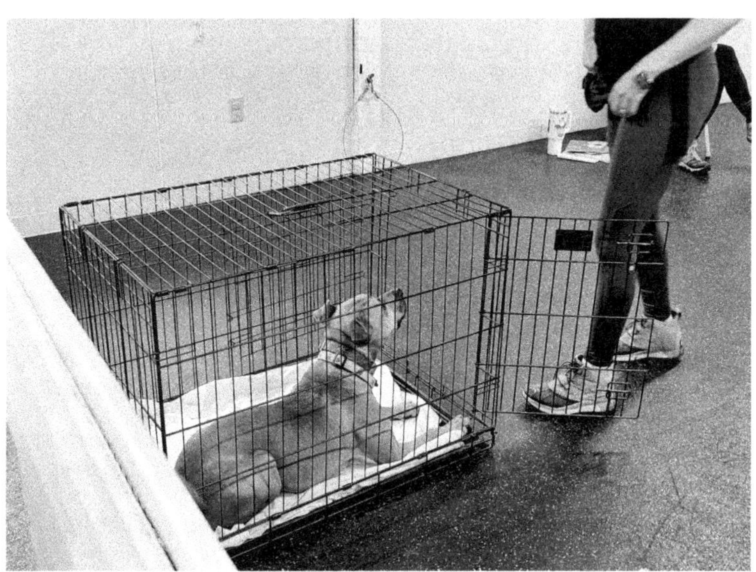

*Imitation Copy.*

**Bonnie Does Phase 1**

I stood in front of Bonnie, told her to, "Wait," and then did the behavior myself (either push the button, step up and sit on the

Stepper, or lie down facing her). Then I returned and gave the "Copy!" cue followed by a pause and then the verbal cue for the behavior I had just performed, without any body-language prompting. In theory the association between repetitions of "Copy!" and the verbal cue for the behavior that was just demonstrated teaches the dog that "Copy!" means "Do whatever I just did." Would it work for Bonnie?

Well ... eventually. Because the behaviors that I had selected for her weren't as solidly on verbal cue as I had hoped (other than the "Down"), we worked through several permutations of "Copy!, Cue," and waiting to see what she did, then prompted. When I could see that she knew what to do before I gave her the cue for the behavior, I stopped using the cue, using only the "Copy" cue after performing the behavior myself. If she offered the correct one, she got a click-and-treat and very happy praise. If she offered an incorrect behavior, I simply reset her, performed the behavior again, returned to stand in front of her and gave the "Copy!" cue. It was exciting to watch as her correct responses gradually began to outnumber the incorrect ones. I could see she was beginning to understand the rule.

I had watched several dogs try to learn the rule on the *Do As I Do* DVD. Some were brilliant, apparently grasping the imitation rule after just a couple of sessions. Others were still struggling at the end of the two-day seminar. Of course, I assumed Bonnie would exhibit the "brilliant" end of the rule-learning continuum, but in all honesty, she was more just slightly toward the brilliant side of center. Or maybe I was the one who was less than brilliant; it was easy to see on the DVD that the dogs with the more skillful trainers learned the rule more quickly. Hmm....

In my defense, the trainers on the DVD had Claudia herself coaching them. In contrast, I was stumbling around on my own, trying to remember what I had watched and occasionally hearing Claudia in my mind's ear saying, "Mmmm. ... You gestured with your eyes!," when I caught myself glancing at the "Easy" button along with my "Copy!" cue.

Nevertheless, despite my ineptitude, Bonnie did seem to catch on to the imitation rule after three days, with several sessions per day. Although we weren't flawless, we were about 90% by the end of the third day; nine out of ten times when I would perform the behavior myself, return to stand in front of her and then give her the "Copy!" cue, she would perform the behavior. She was ready to start Phase 2!

### Imitation: Phase 2

For Phase 2, the steps are very similar to Phase 1 except now you are introducing three new behaviors that your dog already knows. They do not have to be as solidly on verbal cue, since your dog has already grasped the concept, and you are now generalizing it to three more behaviors. Using the same steps, practice Copy with just the three new behaviors until your dog is solid with those, then integrate them with your three Phase 1 behaviors until she is 80% correct or better with all six in random order. On to Phase 3!

### Imitation: Phase 3

Now for the big leap forward—you are going to ask your dog to imitate behaviors that you have not already taught her to do. Wow. Yes, WOW! Using the same steps as Phase 1, pick a new, unknown behavior and go for it. We do know that behaviors with props can be a little easier for our dogs to connect with, so you might try one with a prop first—but then no holds barred, the sky's the limit! Then start thinking about how you can use this in your dog's training programs. How much easier just to show her—and have her do it right away—than spend all that time luring or shaping?

I won't bore you with all of Bonnie's Phase 2 and Phase 3 work, but I will tell you that her very first Phase 3 behavior was to pick up a wicker picnic basket by the handle. She did it perfectly on the second try—and I had never taught her how to pick up anything! So, what can your dog do?

By the way, Claudia just recently released a new study in which she trained dogs to imitate human behavior by watching a video. Oh my … does this mean we may be able to someday train our dogs by sitting them in front of the television to watch training videos? I hope not—training is about relationship!

# Chapter 14

# Cooperative Care Using Agency and Cognition in Husbandry Practices

Up to this point in the book, I have focused on the amazing cognitive abilities of dogs and how you can take that knowledge and apply it to training and building a stronger relationship with your dog. As I am sure you have noticed, there has been an emphasis on having fun and playing games. After all, I wrote a whole book called *Play With Your Dog* several years ago so you can imagine I'm a fan of having fun!

So while it is fun to see the amazing things your dog can be trained to do, your dog can experience pain and remember how it happened, express fearful emotions, and have the seemingly uncanny ability to know that this leads to that. I'm sure you have seen this with your own dogs who don't enjoy going to the groomer. They know what is going to happen and react accordingly. This can be magnified on a visit to the vet!

The good news is that in recent years there has been movement on the part of enlightened vets, dog trainers and owners to work cooperatively to minimize the stress that so many dogs experience when they go to the groomer or a veterinary clinic. This chapter, while it may not be all fun and games, should give you the ability to improve that part of your dog's life.

## Agency in husbandry practices

Sadly, it has long been common practice in the animal care and training world to use forcible restraint when a dog, cat, goat, sheep, even a 1000-pound-plus horse, tries to tell us that they aren't comfortable with whatever procedure we're attempting to impose upon them. This could be vaccinating, medicating, grooming, shearing, nail or hoof trimming or any one of a long list of other things we do to our animal companions. Is it any wonder that for many dogs each subsequent visit to the veterinarian becomes more stressful and requires increasingly more coercive/aversive restraint techniques in order to get the job done?

The good news is that animal care and training professionals are becoming more and more aware of the importance of cooperative care. This growing awareness among force-free animal care professionals means that more and more trainers are adding cooperative care protocols to their puppy social and adult dog good manners classes, coaching their private clients, and offering workshops and seminars, all with the goal of giving our dogs better husbandry experiences as well as making life easier for those who live and work with dogs. There will probably always be those humans—both professional and non-professional—who assume they have the right to do anything they want to our non-human animal companions. However, the ever-increasing numbers of force-free professionals means that those guardians who understand and value the importance of agency and cooperative care now have better choices available to them. Now they can find trainers, behavior professionals, veterinarians, groomers, pet sitters and other animal caretakers who respect our furred, feathered, finned and scaled friends' needs to have agency in their lives.

To that end, Dr. Marty Becker has started an entire Fear Free™ industry, whose mission is "to prevent and alleviate fear, anxiety, and stress in pets by inspiring and educating the people who care for them." Founded in 2016, Fear Free now certifies veterinarians, veterinary practices, trainers, groomers, pet sitters, boarding and daycare facilities and offers a Fear Free animal shelter program. The late Sophia Yin's *Low Stress Handling, Restraint and Behavior Modification* was another pioneering effort to make visits to the vet less stressful.

Other books on this subject can be found in the Recommended Reading list at the end of this book.

## Cooperative care procedures

There are some basic behavioral strategies you can implement that don't require a lot of training, and then there are some more complex protocols that really open lines of communication and consent between you and your canine pal. Here are the easier ones:

### Stay with your dog

There is now at least one study that confirms what many of us have long said: It is better for your dog if you stay with him during your vet visit. My rule—my dogs *never* go "to the back" without me for *any* procedure. The only time they are out of my sight is if they have to stay overnight at the clinic for surgery. Even for radiographs—I escort my dog to the room; help get them on the table and just duck out long enough for the x-rays to be taken (and hopefully the room has a window I can watch through). If I had my dogs professionally groomed (I don't!), being able to stay with them during the grooming session would also be a requirement for me. I would have to stay and watch, preferably in the same room, but at least watching through a window with an agreed-upon signal if I needed to halt whatever is happening at any given time.

A couple of years ago we took our Kelpie, Kai, to a dermatologist to determine what he was allergic to (major skin/itching). After the initial exam during which Kai was, as usual, completely calm and cooperative the vet said, "Okay, now we're going to take him to the back to draw blood." We said, "No you're not." She looked a little startled, but she acquiesced. She said, "Okay, we have one vet tech in the hospital who is willing to do a blood draw in front of the guardians. I will have to go find her." It took about fifteen minutes, but the tech came, drew blood and commented on what a very good boy Kai was. (I also held off the vein for the tech, which my own vets usually let me do with my dogs because they know my history and experience.)

## The least restraint is the best restraint

If your dog is a very good dog like Kai, minimal restraint is always preferred. Several years ago, our Corgi, Lucy, was having anal gland issues. We had her at our vet clinic for an exam and our appointment was with a new vet (from Russia!) for the clinic. (We always get to educate new vets about our acceptable handling practices.) The vet asked if Lucy needed to be restrained for him to be able to examine her nether regions and I said, "Probably not if I feed her treats. …" The vet answered, "Well then, you just keep feeding her those treats!" I did, the exam went well, and I was very appreciative that I didn't have to argue with the vet about it!

If you are capable and your dog is calm and your vet will allow it, it is much less stressful for your dog for you to use whatever minimal restraint is needed, rather than a vet tech bear hug. Of course, vet and staff safety is a high priority, so if your dog is going to present a safety risk or if you aren't skilled at restraint, then the tech should probably do it (while you feed treats!). If your dog is having a hard time, a Fear Free™ vet is likely to suggest that if it's not an urgent procedure you go home with your dog and work on some cooperative care protocols so they can give the vaccination or draw blood *without* a major struggle—while at the same time you teach your dog to love a muzzle in case he needs to wear one for future visits. (Obviously, if there is an urgent need then they will need to do whatever they need to do to stop the bleeding or otherwise treat the emergency.)

## Happy vet visits

I suggest to my clients that they do "Happy Vet Visits" with their dogs. From puppyhood on if the only time your dog goes to the vet is for shots and exams, getting restrained, poked and prodded every visit, it's no wonder that he develops an increasingly negative association with the vet hospital and the vet clinic staff and becomes increasingly more resistant to handling on each subsequent visit. What if instead, for every one visit that involves poking and prodding, he gets multiple visits that involve treats, petting, and just hanging out and relaxing for a while? You can ask your clinic for permission to do this. Most are more than delighted to help give their canine clients a happier association with the vet hospital and the humans who work there. Find out when they aren't very busy so you're not dealing with a crowd in the waiting room, and if possible, include hanging out in an unoccupied exam room as well as the lobby. Have the receptionists, techs and vets poke their noses in and offer your dog some yummy treats. "What a great place!" your dog thinks, "*Everybody* feeds me treats here!"

### Muzzle training

Sometimes dogs need to be muzzled for the safety of the humans who interact with them. There is great value in teaching your dog to love a muzzle. If the only time he is muzzled is when scary/aversive things happen, he will hate the muzzle and he will be even more stressed if he has to wear it for the vet or the groomer. If you can convince him that the muzzle makes good stuff happen, it will be far less stressful for him if there does come a time when he needs to be muzzled for staff safety. (Even Kai might be induced to bite if he is injured and in a lot of pain.) Here's how:

1. **Purchase a top-quality basket muzzle.** (See My Favorite Muzzles below.) Good basket muzzles allow your dog to breathe, pant, eat and drink, which reduces muzzle-related stress and prevents overheating. Measure your dog to ensure a perfect fit; most muzzle websites include a sizing chart that will help you take proper measurements and order the proper size. The best sites will custom fit your dog's muzzle. For additional information about how to find the right muzzle for your dog, check out the **MuzzleUp! Project**.
2. **Show your dog the muzzle**. Don't even try to put it on yet! Just hold it up, then feed your dog a yummy treat from the other hand. Hide your treat hand and muzzle behind your back, then show it to him again and feed. You can also incorporate toys—if your dog loves to chase a ball or a toy, show him the muzzle then throw the toy. If he loves tug, show him the muzzle and play tug. Cool—a muzzle makes toys and tug happen! Repeat this step until, when you bring the muzzle out from behind your back her eyes light up and she looks for the treat or the toy. She now thinks muzzle = yummy/fun stuff!

3. **Feed treats in the muzzle.** Hold the muzzle in one hand and show your dog you have treats in your other hand. You can push high-value treats through the front of the muzzle or use squeeze cheese through the straps; the important part here is that your dog puts her nose into the muzzle voluntarily, you do not push the muzzle onto her nose. If she backs away don't follow her with the muzzle, wait for her to come back to you. You can still toss a toy or play tug after she puts her nose in the muzzle.
4. **Increase the duration**. When your dog voluntarily offers to put her nose into the muzzle (ideally shoves her nose into the muzzle) gradually increase duration by feeding, pausing, then feeding again several times while she keeps her nose in the muzzle. Then toss a toy or play tug, if those are even more reinforcing to your dog than the treats.
5. **Play with the straps**. Now, while holding the muzzle with one hand and occasionally feeding treats, play with the straps a little behind your dog's head as if you are getting ready to buckle it.
6. **Condition your dog to the sound of the snap**. If your muzzle has a snap rather than a buckle and your dog might startle at the sound of the snap, take time to condition her to the sound separately from putting the muzzle on. Hold it up so she can see it, snap the snap in place and feed her a treat or toss the toy—until the sound of the snap makes her eyes light up and she looks for the treat or the toy.
7. **Close the snap or buckle briefly with the muzzle on**. This can be tricky. For starters, how do you keep feeding treats while using two hands to close the snap or buckle? Perhaps you have a partner who can help by feeding the treats while you manipulate the hardware. If not, you can smear peanut butter or squeeze cheese on your refrigerator door or on a vinyl floor to keep your dog happily occupied while you snap or buckle. Alternatively, try the Chase 'n Chomp Sticky Bone® or a Licky Mat® with suction cups, which can suction onto your floor, wall, or refrigerator door.

8. **Leave the muzzle on for longer periods**. Gradually leave the muzzle on your dog for longer periods, making sure to keep her happy (feed treats!) while it's on. Over time you can reduce the frequency of treats or play, but always be ready to treat or toss/tug the toy occasionally to keep it happy for her.
9. **Refresh the positive association**. Be sure to do "happy muzzle" sessions routinely so she doesn't only wear the muzzle for bad/scary times. Once you have conditioned her to love her muzzle, if she wears it only for trips to the vet's office her association will change from positive to negative and you'll have to start all over again. A good rule of thumb: Give your dog at least ten happy muzzle experiences for every stressful one.
10. **Find additional resources**. There is an outstanding YouTube video by superb trainer Chirag Patel (of Domesticated Manners in London, United Kingdom). It is an excellent tutorial for teaching your dog to love a muzzle. (See Recommended Reading and Resources.) Check out the Muzzle Up! Project for more helpful information on muzzling. Support small businesses like Trust Your Dog, who make custom fit muzzles for dogs.

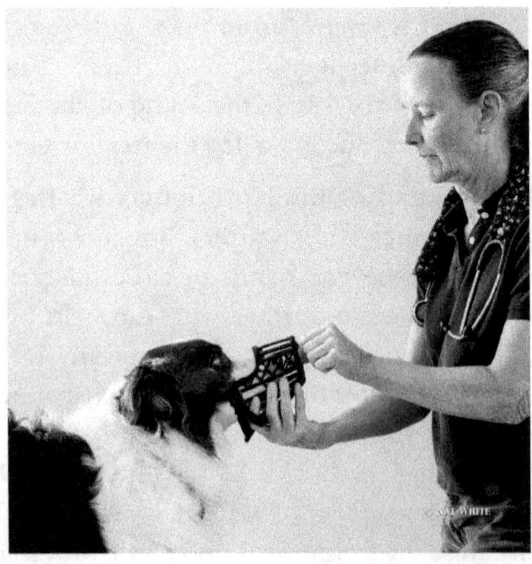

*You want your dog to love his muzzle!*

**My favorite muzzles**

**The Baskerville Ultra Muzzle.** The Baskerville Ultra Muzzle is widely known for security and comfort. The rubber material can actually be heated up and molded to better fit the shape of your dog's face.

**The Bumas Muzzle:** The Bumas Muzzle is made to order. It can be customized with fewer or more straps (depending on your dog's anatomy and the level of security needed) and you can specify the color of each strap on the muzzle. It is especially helpful for **brachycephalic** (flat-faced) dogs who can be difficult to fit.

**Trust Your Dog Muzzle:** These are also good. https://trust-your-dog.com/

Okay now, time to get to work (play)! Check out our favorite muzzles, measure your dog, order one, and start convincing him that it's the best thing since chopped chicken!

## Cooperative care protocols

In addition to the procedures described above that can help your dog have much better handling experiences, the dog behavior and care world is implementing cognitive **cooperative care** protocols where your dog can clearly communicate to you whether he is comfortable with you (or your vet or groomer) proceeding with whatever you are doing. Once you teach him one of these protocols, if he asks you to stop, you must stop until he gives you permission to continue. Therefore, you only use these procedures when you can honor his request to stop. If you're going to use them with your vet or groomer, they have to be willing to honor his requests also. The Chin Rest and the Bucket Game are the two protocols which are in increasingly common usage in the Fear Free™ and force-free world.

### The Chin Rest

The Chin Rest has been in use for many years. While its origin appears to have been lost, it is closely related to a number of behaviors used in wild animal parks—teaching animals such as bears and dolphins to target a specific body part to a designated spot for husbandry purposes. Remember that zookeepers taught a Sun Bear to his open mouth to the bars of his cage so they could do the exam without having to sedate the bear. The chin rest is very similar—first teach your dog to target his chin to a rolled-up towel or your cupped hands and hold it there for long duration. You then teach the cognitive part—you want him to understand the concept that resting his chin is giving you permission to proceed with whatever you are doing and lifting his chin is his request for you to stop.

I much prefer teaching the Chin Rest to a rolled-up towel placed on a chair or other surface rather than my hands, because I want my hands to be free so I can administer whatever husbandry procedure I'm working on. You can *also* teach with the dog's chin on your hands as well as the towel on the chair—and this may be useful/reassuring to your dog if his chin is in your hands while your vet is doing a procedure. Here's the procedure:

**Teaching the towel Chin Rest:**

1. Place a rolled-up towel (taped so it doesn't unroll) on a chair or stool. You can also tape it to the chair or stool to prevent it from moving around.
2. Shape or lure your dog to touch her chin to the towel. You may click or use a verbal marker when the chin makes contact, but it's not necessary. He can be sitting or standing or even lying down if that works best for you.
3. Ask your dog to hold chin contact for one second, then two seconds, etc. Gradually as the duration of his chin rest begins increasing, reward him with treats for longer and longer periods. Don't wait too long, increasing the duration too much, too quickly may cause the behavior to extinguish. Remember this is a game of choice; your dog is allowed to look around between resting his chin. Let your dog choose to participate.
4. Practice until your dog is able to hold his chin on the towel for a duration of at least ten seconds. Remember that it doesn't matter what position he's in; it could be a sit, down or stand. Remember this is a game of choice; your dog is allowed to lift his chin. The reinforcement for the chin lift is that you stop doing whatever you were doing when he lifted his chin. (Negative reinforcement.)

*The Chin Rest.*

## Introducing the concept of choice and control

1. Choose what procedure you want to introduce to your dog first as part of the Chin Rest, such as being groomed or looking in his ears or mouth. I'll describe the steps as if we were working on brushing the dog.

2. When he is resting his chin and can hold it for at least ten seconds, start moving your hand toward his side (not touching him). If he continues to rest his chin, stop moving your hand toward him and feed him a treat. If he lifts his chin, probably to look at your hand or face ("What are you doing?"), just draw your hand back. Don't say anything. Remember this is a game of choice. He may not yet understand that he can communicate to you that he is uncomfortable—he may have just been curious, but he will come to understand and apply the cognitive concept of choice as you continue the process.

3. When he places his chin back on the towel, the game begins again. This time don't move your hand so fast or far. If he keeps his chin on the towel, reward him with a treat. Repeat this process with your hand moving toward him, closer and closer, giving him a treat every so often as long as he continues to rest his chin and always withdraw your hand if he lifts his head.

4. Eventually you should be able to touch him as he keeps his chin on the towel. The first time you make contact with him he will likely look at you. Just withdraw your hand and try again after he rests his chin. He should be starting to figure out that the only way to get treats is to keep his chin on the towel no matter what you do with your hand. Touch him with increasing pressure at various locations on his body where you will be grooming him, rewarding him with a treat every so often. Again, don't wait so long that he starts to think it's not worth playing the game, but eventually he should be able to hold his chin on the towel for at least ten to fifteen seconds while you touch him.
5. Now pick up his brush and repeat Step 3, this time with the brush in your hand. After several repetitions with the brush held near him, start touching him with the brush. This continues until you are able to groom your dog while he continues to rest his chin on the towel.

To teach your dog to Chin Rest to your hands use the same procedure, just substitute your hands for the towel and have someone else do the gradually increasing movements and contact.

### The Bucket Game

The Bucket Game was developed and introduced to the dog training world more recently, also by the previously mentioned trainer Chirag Patel, owner of Domesticated Manners, a training business in London. Once taught, the Bucket Game can be used for the same long list of husbandry procedures, including veterinary exams, administering medication, grooming and nail trimming. Remember that you *have to* honor your dog's request.

This fun and easy dog-training protocol empowers the learner by creating an environment where your dog has choice and can communicate his willingness to participate. Using the Bucket Game, your dog can tell you:

- When he is ready to start
- When he needs to take a break

- When he wants to stop
- When you need to slow down

All you need to play the Bucket Game is a small bucket or some other container to hold treats, and a lot of small, high-value treats.

### Teaching impulse control in the presence of the bucket

1. Start by holding the bucket (with treats in it) out to your side. You can rattle it if necessary to get your dog to look at it. Reward your dog (feed a treat from the bucket) for looking at the bucket but maintaining some distance from it (two to four feet). Usually, once your dog has seen you reach into the bucket, take out a yummy treat, and feed it to him, he'll look at the bucket again, wondering what it's all about. Be ready! When you see him glance at it, take a treat out of it and give him one. (You can use a clicker or verbal marker to mark the behavior if you like, but it's not necessary.) You're on your way. Repeat a few times. If your dog tries to jump up or dive into the bucket don't admonish him; just raise it higher. It shouldn't take long for him to realize that the best way to get more treats is to keep returning his gaze to the bucket without trying to jump up and help himself to them.
2. Put the bucket on the ground, a chair, or a table and reward the dog (feed a treat from the bucket) for looking at it but not trying to get it. Your dog can be in any position; you are simply rewarding him for looking at the bucket. You do not want him to move toward it or try to get treats out of the bucket. Repeat several times.
3. Gradually begin increasing the duration of his gaze by rewarding him with treats from the bucket for looking at it for longer and longer periods. Don't wait too long, increasing the duration too much, too quickly, as this may cause the behavior to extinguish. **Extinction** happens when a behavior is no longer reinforced (or when the reinforcement rate is too low) and the dog doesn't see any reason to offer the behavior. Like, you stop going to work if your employer stops paying you! Remember this is a game of choice; your dog is allowed to look around

between focusing on the bucket. Don't call his name, tap on the bucket, or do anything else to draw his attention to it. Let your dog choose to engage in participating.

**Introducing the concept of choice and control**

1. Practice until your dog is able to focus on the bucket for a duration of at least ten seconds. Remember that it doesn't matter what position he's in; it could be a sit, down or stand.
2. Choose what procedure you want to introduce to your dog first as part of the Bucket Game, such as being groomed or looking in his ears. I'll describe the steps as if we were working on brushing the dog.
3. When he is focused on the bucket and able to hold his focus for at least ten seconds, start moving your hand toward his side (not touching him). If he continues to look at the bucket, stop moving your hand toward him and feed him a treat from the bucket. If he looks away from the bucket, probably to look at your hand or face (wondering "What are you doing?"), just draw your hand back. Don't say anything. Remember this is a game of choice. He may not yet understand that he can communicate to you that he is uncomfortable—he may have just been curious, but he will come to understand and apply the cognitive concept of choice as you continue the process.
4. When he re-engages with the bucket, the game begins again. This time don't move your hand so fast or far. If he is able to maintain focus on the bucket, reward him with a treat from the bucket. Repeat this process with your hand moving toward him, closer and closer, giving him a treat every so often as long as he continues to gaze at the bucket and always withdraw your hand if he looks away from the bucket.
5. Eventually you should be able to touch him as he gazes at the bucket. The first time you make contact with him he will likely look at you. Just withdraw your hand and try again after he gazes at the bucket again. He should be starting to figure out that the only way to get treats is to keep gazing

at the bucket no matter what you do with your hand. Touch him with increasing pressure at various locations on his body where you will be grooming him, rewarding him with a treat every so often. Again, don't wait so long that he starts to think it's not worth playing the game, but eventually he should be able to hold his gaze on the bucket for at least ten or fifteen seconds while you touch him.

6. Now pick up his brush and repeat Step 3, this time with the brush in your hand. After several repetitions with the brush held near him, start touching him with the brush. This continues until you are able to groom your dog with him continuing to look at the bucket.

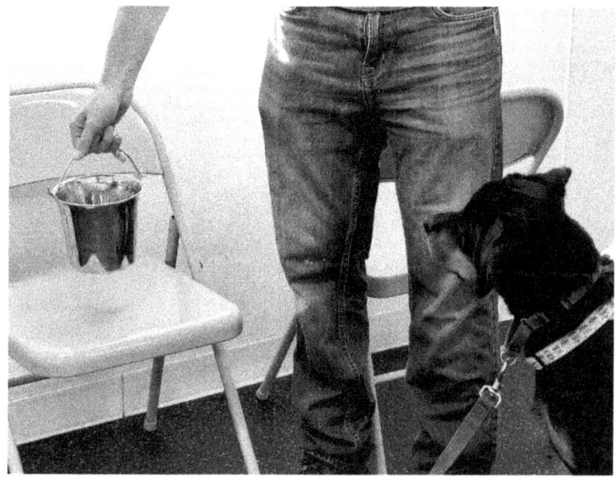

*Teaching the Bucket Game.*

## The most important rule of the games

When your dog has learned either game for one procedure, you can easily generalize it to others, including ear and mouth exams, foot handling, nail trimming, etc.

However, these games of choice and control will only work if you allow your dog to communicate that he wishes to begin, take a break, and stop the game. If your dog looks away from the bucket or lifts his chin, stop the game. When he re-engages with the bucket or rests his chin again, the game continues. It's imperative that you honor his request to stop. Only use the procedure when you are able to honor his request to stop.

If you use the Bucket Game or Chin Rest while working with other animal-care professionals, they also must be willing to stop any procedure when your dog looks away from the bucket or lifts his chin. If they are not willing to do so, don't use the games with them. If they are doing a procedure that cannot be stopped once it has started, don't use the Bucket Game or Chin Rest with that procedure.

You can also enhance your use of these protocols if you utilize a Counter-conditioning and **desensitization** protocol to convince your dog that being touched and handled is a good thing, not a bad thing. You accomplish this by associating being touched with yummy stuff, like chicken. (See: Counter-conditioning and Desensitization (CC&D) on page 137.)

### Bonnie's Bucket Game

Here's the thing. Without a means to communicate peacefully, our dogs are forced to employ **agonistic** (relating to fighting/aggression) behaviors to convey their discomfort with our handling and husbandry. We tend to ignore their lower-level agonistic expressions—tension, avoidance—and so they are forced to escalate to more dramatic behaviors to get their message across. This isn't fun for them either, so they get more and more tense about the procedures as their negative association with them increases. When they have an effective means to communicate calmly and that communication is heard and respected, it takes the tension out of the procedure.

My wonderful dog Bonnie (whom we called a Scorgidoodle, but we never did a DNA test, so we really don't know …) was the sweetest girl in the world. She had long, soft curly hair that clumped easily. Despite my best efforts to keep her groomed, she managed to get small mats in her fur from time to time. She seemed comfortable when I brushed her head, shoulders, front legs and rib cage, but she would get tense when I combed her hindquarters. Although she never came close to biting me, she was clearly becoming more and more unhappy about it as time went on.

Then, over three separate six-day Behavior Modification Academies, my students taught her the Bucket Game. It really was amazing. After the third academy she no longer got tense about the grooming and apparently didn't even seem to feel the need to ask me to stop. It seemed as if just knowing that she *could* ask me to stop and that I would stop if she asked, was enough to take all the tension out of the grooming procedures. She totally made a believer out of me!

*Bonnie's Bucket Game.*

## Counter-Conditioning and Desensitization (CC&D)

Counter-conditioning and Desensitization were both covered in detail in Chapter 4: How Dogs Learn. You may want to go review that again. I am including parts of it here as the concepts may be of value to your dog for the various husbandry procedures she will encounter throughout her life. We will look at the example of nail clipping here. Many of the husbandry issues your dog might encounter would be dealt with in a similar fashion. Although she might think, "It's scary when someone holds my paw to clip my nails," we want to convince her that having someone hold her paw makes good stuff happen—like yummy chicken!

Before you begin, determine your dog's **threshold**, which is the location and duration your dog can be touched and handle touching without reacting fearfully or aggressively. Perhaps it's her shoulder, perhaps her elbow or maybe her knee. She should be a little worried, but not growl or try to move away. Then follow these steps:

1. With your dog on leash, touch her briefly and gently at threshold. The instant your dog notices the touch, start feeding bits of chicken non-stop. Keep your chicken hand behind your back when you aren't feeding so she doesn't just gaze adoringly at it.
2. After a second or two, remove the touch and stop feeding chicken. Keep repeating the first two steps until touching at that location for one to two seconds consistently causes your dog to look at you with a happy smile and a "Yay! Where's my chicken?" expression. This is a conditioned emotional response (CER)—your dog's association with the brief touch at that location is now **appetitive** (your dog wants to move towards the touch) instead of **aversive** (your dog wants to move away from the touch).
3. Now you need to increase the intensity of the stimulus by increasing the length of time you touch her at that same location a few seconds at a time, obtaining a new +CER at each new time period before increasing the time again. For example, several repetitions at two to four seconds until you get consistent "Yay!" looks, then several repetitions at four to eight seconds, then several at eight to twelve seconds, etc., working for that consistent +CER at each new duration of your touch.
4. Increase the intensity of the stimulus again, this time by moving your hand to a new location one to two inches lower than your initial threshold. If you started at the shoulder, touch her there, and slide your hand down an inch toward her paw. I suggest starting at your initial touch location and sliding your hand to the new spot rather than just touching the new spot. Continue with repetitions until you get consistent +CERs at the new location.

5. Continue gradually working your way down to your dog's paw an inch or two at a time, getting solid CERs at each spot before you move closer to the paw.
6. When you get below the knee, also add a gentle grasp and a little pressure to the procedure—each a separate step in the CC&D process. Do multiple repetitions of pressure just below the knee, and when she's happy with that, slide your hand and do CC&D an inch lower. When she's good with that, add pressure. Continue an inch at a time until you are all the way down to the paw, be sure to get the "Yay!" response with touch before you add the grasp, and then with grasp, before you add pressure. Continue working down the leg all the way to the paw.
7. When you can touch, grasp and put pressure on the paw, add lifting the paw.
8. If your goal is happy nail trimming, start the process over, this time with the nail clipper in your hand. Show her the clippers, feed a treat, until the appearance of the clippers elicits a "Yay!" response. Then do CC&D with the clipper action—squeezing the clippers to make the sound and motion it would make if you were actually clipping nails.
9. Go through the whole touch sequence again, this time with the clippers in your hand, also touching her with the clippers, then again while you squeeze the clippers. Remember that you are still feeding yummy treats and obtaining CERs along the way throughout the whole process. When you can hold her paw and make the clipper action right next to her nail and see a happy response, clip one nail, feed lots of treats, and stop. Do a nail a day until she's happy with that, then advance to two nails at a time, then three, until you can clip all her nails in one setting.

The more complex the stimulus, the more successful the dog's avoidance or aggressive strategies have been, and the more intense the response, the more challenging the behavior is to modify. Take your time. As we say in the dog training world, "In behavior modification, if you think you're going too slow … slow down!"

# Chapter 15

## Bringing it All Home

## Brain Candy and Your Relationships with All Species

---

By now you should have plenty of great ideas about how to incorporate fun cognition games to enrich your life and relationship with your canine companion(s). This chapter will summarize the cognitive exercises we've detailed in the previous chapters and give you some additional ideas for real-life applications. Then (surprise!) we'll share some thoughts about playing cognition games with *other* species who may share your home and heart.

### Agency: Choice and Control

Remember that Dr. Susan Friedman tells us, "The power to control one's own outcomes is essential to behavioral health." I often think lack of choice could be a significant contributor to the escalation of behavior challenges we're seeing in today's dogs. Now that you have taught your dog the *concept* of choice, let's look at different ways you can incorporate this in his life to help improve his behavioral health. Here are some ideas:

- You're shopping with your dog at your favorite pet supply store. Pick up two toys, have your dog Sit and Wait, offer both toys and say, "You choose!" (Of course you have to buy the one he chooses.)

- You fix his dinner and prepare two different toppings—maybe one chicken flavor, one beef flavor. Offer him the toppings in two separate bowls, name each bowl as you let him sniff it and then offer both and say, "You choose!" Put that one on his dinner and feed him.
- You're walking in the woods and the path divides. Have your dog sit facing the trails and you face him. Name each trail, left and right *(his left and right)* and then say, "You choose!" Go the way he chooses.
- Hold up a toy and his leash. Say "Play Ball or Go for a walk? You choose!" Honor his choice.

Now *you* think up some that will work for you and your dog. Remember—the more ways you can find to give your dog choices in his life, the better it is for his behavioral health—and we all want behaviorally healthy dogs!

**Talking buttons**

By the way ... you may have noticed that I didn't include anything in this book about those talking buttons that allegedly allow a dog to express his thoughts and feelings and are now the rage in parts of the dog-owning population. The reason I didn't is because so far there is no scientific evidence that dogs are actually doing that. There is one very recent study that demonstrates that dogs can understand and respond appropriately to cues from the talking button (i.e., the button says, "Sit" and the dog sits; the button says, "Outside" and the dog goes to the door) which shouldn't surprise anyone. But so far, the general consensus in both the behavior science world and the professional training and behavior fields is that any attempt to assign a dog's thoughts and feelings to the buttons is simply human interpretation with no real basis to confirm validity of the dog's alleged expression of thoughts and feelings. Sorry gang!

## Consent and Cooperative Care

Consent is another area relevant to Choice that is also critical to your dog's behavioral health. Unless it is completely unavoidable (i.e., a medical emergency) you want to always be able to give your dog the option to opt out of interacting with another dog, a human, or any other species, for that matter.

**With dogs**. Create controlled introductions with other dogs whenever possible. I know, sometimes an off-leash dog comes charging up to you—that's a whole different issue! If that happens and your dog is okay with it, let them interact. If the other dog appears threatening or your dog is not comfortable with the other dog, make an emergency exit as quickly as possible.

For a controlled meeting, I recommend having dogs on leashes on opposite sides of an enclosed space. Try to keep leashes loose if possible. The dogs should seem interested in each other, alert without excessive arousal, ideally with tails wagging at half-mast; soft, wriggling body postures; play bows; ears back; squinty eyes; no direct eye contact. These are clear expressions of non-aggressive social invitation.

If you see appropriate social behavior, proceed with an approach until the dogs are about ten feet apart. Now do some parallel walking, staying six to ten feet apart. If they continue to show unambiguous signs of friendliness, drop the leashes and let them meet. I prefer to let dogs meet and greet without leash restraint; leashes tend to interfere with the dogs' ability to greet normally and can actually induce dogs to give false body language signals that might cause an aggressive response from the other dog. It can also increase stress in the restrained dog which can also trigger aggression in the leashed dog—aggression is caused by stress.

On the other hand, if you see agonistic body language including stiffness, standing tall, leaning forward, ears pricked hard forward, growling, hard direct eye contact, stiffly raised, fast-wagging tails, lunging on the leash and aggressive barking, you know it's probably not going to go well.

Alternatively, you may see avoidance behavior—your dog turns away, tries to move away, moves behind you … If you see any of these signs your dog is telling you he does not want to meet/greet this dog. Respect his choice—he does not have to be friends with every dog he sees!

If these are two dogs who eventually will have to be sharing the same living space, proceed very slowly, seek help from a force-free trainer and behavior professional if necessary, only allowing the dogs to actually interact when both are clearly happily willing to do so.

**With humans**. Again, your dog is not required to meet and greet every human who wants to say hi to him. If your dog rushes right up with a happy tail-wagging greeting, fine, go for it! If, however, he appears at all cautious or reluctant, have the human sit or kneel sideways to your dog, advise them *not* to reach toward him, and let the dog approach if he chooses. If he warms up to the person, they can lay their hand with their knuckles on their knee, palm up and let the dog make contact if he so chooses, only working up to petting if and when the dog is clearly inviting interaction—soft body language, nudging the hand, pushing into the person, resting his head on their hand or knee, etc.

All continued or escalated interactions are at the dog's discretion—even if the initial meeting was happy, he is free to leave at any point when he has had enough. Consent Test! If he doesn't want to approach a human at all and they really want some dog interaction, you can have them toss treats away from themselves (not trying to tempt him to come closer). If he begins to relax, they can gradually toss a few treats closer—but the goal is not to have him come up and be petted, unless and until he clearly indicates the desire to do so. Of course, he is still free to disconnect whenever he chooses.

## Husbandry procedures

As your dog's advocate, it is your responsibility to ensure that he is handled and treated appropriately for all husbandry, handling and training procedures. Fear-Free™ and true force-free professionals are supposed to follow this ethic, but sadly, some do not. This is why I never leave my dog unattended in the hands of someone else unless I am 200% sure that they are 100% force-free. My dogs don't *ever* go to the "back room" at the vet hospital, and I would never leave them at the groomer's while I run to the grocery store—I am right there with them the whole time. You should feel free to intervene if at any time *anyone*—a behavior professional, a veterinarian, a groomer, a pet-sitter, the President of the United States—tries to do anything to your dog that you are not comfortable with—I don't care who they are.

The more you can incorporate cognitive protocols into your dog's routines, the easier it will be to take care of his needs without drama or trauma. The Bucket Game and Chin Rest are ideal protocols for giving your dog agency over husbandry procedures and well worth the effort.

## Brain Candy Games

All of the Brain Candy games described in the previous chapters can enrich your life with your dog and greatly enhance his quality of life. They are worth doing just for the entertainment value as well as the joy they add to your relationship. And they don't have to just be for show! Yes, you can WOW the residents of the nursing home where you take him for your Therapy Dog outings and your child can be the star of Show and Tell at his school. But you can also use Discrimination and Nose Games to teach him to find your lost phone or car keys, and Imitation to teach him an endless list of new, complex behaviors. Imagine teaching your dog Service Dog tasks easily, just by having him watch you turn on a light, open a door, pull off a sock and more. Or putting the empty soda can in the recycling bin. Or running the Weave Poles flawlessly on your Agility course. With Match to Sample, you can ask him to bring you the object that is the same as the one that you show him. Better still, you can combine several of the Games to ask him to bring you your yellow scarf from the laundry room or take the blue shoes from the kitchen to your son in the bedroom. The possibilities are endless and as we dive even deeper into our exploration and understanding of the cognitive capabilities of non-human animals, I have no doubt that we will find yet more ways to work with the amazing brains of the species that share our planet. Stay tuned. …

Speaking of the cognitive abilities of non-human animals, we really are just beginning to appreciate those. We know that horses can recognize human faces and voices, they are able to plan ahead and think strategically, solve problems and play Discrimination Games and no doubt much more. Cats are capable of complex thinking and problem solving and can also learn cognition games. Birds can count and make tools, problem solve and more. In fact, I'm willing to bet that pretty much every species on earth is more cognitive than we've given them credit for in the past. Heck, scientists are even telling us that insects are cognitive. In the end, doesn't that all make sense? If creatures weren't cognitive—able to problem-solve, remember, and able to learn and apply concepts how could they survive? While it is not a life and death decision. your dog might think "It's scary when someone holds my paw to clip my nails." We want to convince her that having someone hold her paw makes good stuff happen—like yummy chicken!

So go now and enjoy your cognition journey with your canine companion while you enhance quality of life for both of you. While you're at it, don't forget your cat. And your horse. And …

*Teaching Samuel the mule Color Discrimination.*

# Recommended Reading and Resources

## Books

Abramson, Charles I. *Selected Papers and Biography of Charles Henry Turner 1867-1923: Pioneer of Comparative Animal Behavior Studies (Black Studies)*. Edwin Mellen Pr., 2002. Heavy scientific read.

Albrecht, Kat. *Dog Detectives: Train Your Dog to Find Lost Pets*. Dogwise Publishing, 20027. Easy, engaging read.

Bender, Allie and Emily Strong. *Canine Enrichment for the Real World: Making it a Part of Your Dog's Daily Life*. Dogwise Publishing, 2019. Medium read. There is a companion workbook as well: *Canine Enrichement for the Real World Workbook*, 2022.

Bergin ED. D., Bonnie and Sharon Hogan. *Teach Your Dog to Read: A Unique Step-by-Step Program to Expand Your Dog's Mind and Strengthen the Bond Between You*. Broadway, 2006. Easy read.

Berns, Gregory. *How Dogs Love Us: A Neuroscientist and His Adopted Dog Decode the Canine Brain*. Amazon Publishing, 2022. Somewhat scientific, medium read.

Fisher, Gail Tamases. *The Thinking Dog: Crossover to Clicker Training*. Dogwise Publishing, 2009. Medium read.

Fugazza, Claudia and Fumi Higaki. *Do As I Do: Using Social Learning to Train Dogs, 2nd Edition*. Dogwise Publishing, 2014, 2024). Easy read.

Hare, Brian and Vanessa Woods. *The Genius of Dogs: How Dogs Are Smarter Than You Think*. Plume, 2013. Easy, fascinating read.

Harrington, Janice N. (author), Taylor III, Theodore (illustrator). *Buzzing with Questions: The Inquisitive Mind of Charles Henry Turner.* Calkins Creek, 2019. For young readers.

Horowitz, Alexandra. *Inside of a Dog: What Dogs See, Smell and Know.* Scribner, 2010. Medium, a little sciency.

Horowitz, Alexandra. *Domestic Dog Cognition and Behavior: The Scientific Study of Canis familiaris*. Springer, 2014. Scientific, dense read.

Horowitz, Alexandra. *Being a Dog: Following the Dog Into a World of Smell.* Scribner, 2016. Easy read.

Kokias, Kerri (author), Lowery, Mike (illustrator). *Clever Hans: The True Story of the Counting, Adding, and Time-Telling Horse.* G.P. Putnam's Sons, 2020. Young readers.

Miklosi, Adam. *Dog Behaviour, Evolution, and Cognition,* (2nd edition). Oxford University Press, 2016. Scientific, dense read.

Miller, Pat. *Play With Your Dog.* Dogwise Publishing, 2008. Easy read.

Miller, Pat. and Leslie Sinn, DVM. *Veterinary Cooperative Care: Enhancing Animal Health Through Collaboration with Veterinarians, Pet Owners, and Animal Trainers*. Dogwise Publishing, 2023. Medium, scientific read.

Pfungst, Oskar (author), Rahn, Carl Leo (translator). *Clever Hans (The Horse of Mr. Von Osten): A contribution to experimental animal and human psychology.* CreateSpace Independent Publishing Platform, 2011. Scientific, dense read.

Pienaar, Karin. *Mood Matters: MHERA: An innovative assessment approach to animal emotionality in the treatment of behaviour problems*. Dogwise Publishing, 2022. Medium read.

Pilley, John. *Chaser: Unlocking The Genius of the Dog Who Knows a Thousand Words.* Harvest, 2014. The story of Pilley's deep dive into canine cognition with his Border Collie, Chaser, easy, engaging read.

Ramirez, Ken. *The Eye of the Trainer. Animal Training, Transformation, and Trust.* Karen Pryor Clicker Training, 2020. Medium, engaging scientific read.

Snider, Kellie. *Turning Fierce Dogs Friendly: Using Constructional Aggression Treatment to Rehabilitate Aggressive and Reactive Dogs.* Companion House Books, 2018. Medium, a little sciency read.

Yin, Dr. Sophia. *Low Stress Handling, Restraint and Behavior Modifcation of Dogs and Cats, 2nd edition.* CattleDog Publishing, 2024. Medium read.

## Articles and Studies

Becker, Dr. Marty and Matthew Bubear. "From Pheromones to Animal Housing—How Fear Free is Transforming Companion Animal Practice." *Improve Veterinary Practice*, February 13, 2024. https://www.veterinary-practice.com/article/fear-free-transforming-companion-animal-practice.

Bekoff, Marc. "Animal Emotions: Exploring Passionate Natures: Current interdisciplinary research provides compelling evidence that many animals experience such emotions as joy, fear, love, despair, and grief—we are not alone." *BioScience*, vol. 50, no. 10, October 2000, pp. 861–870.

Goodall, Jane. "This Day in History: Jane Goodall observes a chimpanzee making and using tools." *History.com*, updated June 2, 2023. https://www.history.com/this-day-in-history/jane-goodall-observes-a-chimpanzee-making-and-using-tools.

Horowitz, Alexandra. "Smelling themselves: Dogs investigate their own odours longer when modified in an 'olfactory mirror' test." *Science Direct*, October 2017. https://doi.org/10.1016/j.beproc.2017.08.001.

Jones, Deb. "Shaping; It's Not What You Think It Is." *K9 In Focus* blog. https://k9infocus.com/shaping-its-not-what-you-think-it-is/.

Kaldas, Samuel. "Descartes versus Cudworth On The Moral Worth of Animals." *Philosophy Now*; 2015. https://philosophynow.org/issues/108/Descartes_versus_Cudworth_On_The_Moral_Worth_of_Animals.

Katsnelson, Alla. "Charles Henry Turner's insights into animal behavior were a century ahead of their time." *Knowable Magazine*, August 2, 2023. https://knowablemagazine.org/content/article/living-world/2023/rediscovering-legacy-charles-henry-turner.

Kohda, Masanori, Redouan Bshary and Naoki Kubo. "Cleaner fish recognize self in a mirror via self-face recognition like humans." *Proceedings of the National Academy of Sciences of the United States of America*. Feburary 6, 2023. https://www.pnas.org/doi/10.1073/pnas.2208420120.

McConnell, Patricia, PhD. "Chirag Patel and the 'Bucket Game'." *The Other End of the Leash* blog, 2021. https://www.patriciamcconnell.com/theotherendoftheleash/chirag-patel-and-the-bucket-game.

Miller, Pat. "The Dog's Mind: An interview with Brian Hare, PhD, a leading researcher into canine cognition." *Whole Dog Journal*, April 16, 2, 2013. https://www.whole-dog-journal.com/training/the-dogs-mind.

Pryor, Karen. "101 Things to Do With a Box." 2009, *Karen Pryor Clicker Training*. https://www.clickertraining.com/101-things-to-do-with-a-box.

Steinker, Angelica. "The Art and Science of Consent Testing." *Barks: For Animal Training and Pet Care Professionals* (Pet Professional Guild), January 13, 2022. https://www.petprofessionalguild.com/barks/barks-magazine-blog/the-art-and-science-of-consent-testing/.

Todd, Zazie, PhD. "How to Tell If Your Pet Actually Wants You to Pet Them; Taking a pause for a 'consent test'." *Psychology Today*; March 31, 2022. https://www.psychologytoday.com/us/blog/fellow-creatures/202203/how-to-tell-if-your-pet-actually-wants-you-to-pet-them.

## Links

AKC Tracking competition regulations. https://images.akc.org/pdf/rulebooks/RU9999.pdf

Alexandra Horowitz. https://alexandrahorowitz.net/

Baskerville Muzzle fitting. https://companyofanimals.com/us/brand/baskerville/

Bumas Muzzle. https://bumas-muzzle.com/en/

Concept Training Match-to-Sample Revisited. Ken Ramirez, Karen Pryor Academy, 2020. https://www.facebook.com/KarenPryorAcademy/videos/198330151501586/

"Dog Behaviours in Veterinary Consultations: Part 1. Effect of the owner's presence or absence." https://www.sciencedirect.com/science/article/pii/S109002332200003X?dgcid=author

"Dogs process numerical quantities in similar brain region as humans." A 2019 study conducted at Emory University in Atlanta, Georgia by Lauren Aulet et al. https://news.emory.edu/features/2019/12/esc-dogs-numerical/index.html

Dr. Nathanial Hall, Director of the Canine Olfaction Research and Education Laboratory at Texas Tech University. https://www.depts.ttu.edu/afs/people/nathan-hall/

Dr. Susan G. Friedman, Ph.D., professor emeritus in the Department of Psychology at Utah State University. www.behaviorworks.org/

Fear Free program—find referrals to practitioners near you: https://www.fearfree.com/about-fearfree/

K9 Nosework™. A competitive sport. https://k9nosework.com/

Missing Animal Response Network (MARN). Lost Pet Recovery Training by Kat Albrecht. https://www.missinganimalresponse.com/

"Muzzle Acclimation." Michael Shikashio. https://youtu.be/Q5qsty9s9n0?si=Vbf48Z4Civ0nkcLi

Muzzle Up! Project. https://muzzleupproject.com/

Search and Rescue Dogs of the United States (SARDUS). https://www.facebook.com/Searchdogsus/

Sniffspot. https://www.sniffspot.com/

"Teaching a Dog to Wear a Muzzle." Chirag Patel, Domesticated Manners. https://www.youtube.com/watch?v=1FABgZTFvHo

"The Bucket Game." Chirag Patel, Domesticated Manners. https://www.youtube.com/watch?v=GJSs9eqi2r8

Tool-making crows. https://www.youtube.com/watch?v=TtmLVP0HvDg Caledonian crow making and using a tool; quisling76

# Glossary

**Agency**: The ability to exercise individual control and autonomy in decision-making and actions; The ability to perceive and change the environment, and to select and perform actions to achieve a goal.

**Agonistic**: Social interactions involving conflict, including aggression, threats, and displays of submission in animals.

**Amygdala**: A part of the brain; a major processing center for emotions. The amygdala is primarily associated with fear, but it also plays a role in other emotions like anger, anxiety, and pleasure. It also links emotions to many other brain abilities, especially memories, learning and senses. Malfunction of the amygdala can cause or contribute to disruptive feelings and symptoms.

**Anthropomorphic**: The attribution of human characteristics or behavior to non-human entities, including animals.

**Appetitive**: A pleasant event or stimulus, something the dog would like to have or to do.

**Aversive**: An unpleasant event or stimulus, something the dog would want to avoid.

**Brachycephalic**: Dogs with flat noses—i.e., Pugs, French Bulldogs, English Bulldogs, etc.

**CIPA (Congenital Insensitivity to Pain and Anhydrosis Syndrome)**: A very rare and dangerous autosomal recessive disorder of the nervous system which prevents the feeling of pain or temperature and prevents a person from sweating.

**Classical-conditioning**: A type of learning where a neutral stimulus becomes associated with a naturally occurring stimulus, causing the neutral stimulus to eventually trigger a similar response, essentially learning through association by repeatedly pairing two stimuli together.

**Clicker**: a small handheld device used to communicate with our dogs that they have done exactly what we are looking for. Clickers are precise and consistent, which makes them a valued tool among many trainers.

**Cognition**: The mental processes involved in gaining knowledge and comprehension including (but not limited to) thinking, knowing, remembering, judging, and problem-solving.

**Consciousness**: Awareness of internal and external existence.

**Consent Test**: A process to determine if an individual voluntarily chooses to participate in an interaction or activity.

**Co-operative Care**: Training an animal to not only tolerate handling and husbandry procedures, but to be an active, willing participant in these experiences.

**Counter-conditioning**: The process of changing a previously established association between two stimuli to a new association between those two stimuli.

**Desensitization**: Gradually exposing an individual to a feared object or situation in a controlled and relaxed environment, starting at a low intensity of stimulus and gradually increasing the intensity as the individual habituates to the stimulus at each new level.

**Discrimination (Stimulus Discrimination)**: The ability to distinguish between one stimulus and similar stimuli.

**Distractor Object**: Object used in Match to Sample object that is not the object you are asking the subject to match.

**Enrichment**: acknowledging that dogs have species-specific and breed-specific needs.

**Ethologist**: A scientist who studies the behavior of animals in their natural environment.

**Extinction**: when a behavior is no longer reinforced (or when the reinforcement rate is too low) and the dog doesn't see any reason to offer the behavior.

**Extinguish**: To eliminate a previously reinforced behavior by removing all reinforcement.

**Fast-mapping**: The hypothesized process whereby a new concept (word, name of an object, etc.) is learned based only on minimal exposure.

**Force-free training**: The method of training dogs (or any animal per se) without using force, coercion, threats, intimidation or inflicting pain on the animal. This involves avoiding punishments or anything that invokes fear and panic, causes pain, or harms the dog in any other way.

**Functional Imitation**: Imitation performed in which the copied behavior is a variation (but close proximity) of the original behavior due to physical differences of the subject doing the imitating.

**Indication behavior**: A behavior (either natural or learned) with which the dog communicates to you that he has found or is aware of something; commonly used in scent work and with service dogs.

**Long line**: a 20-to-50-foot leash that allows him to really explore his world.

**Lumping**: In shaping, expecting/reinforcing large increments of behavior rather than small ones. Not recommended.

**Metacognition**: The process of thinking about one's own thinking, or the knowledge and understanding of one's own thought processes.

**Missing Animal Response Network ™**: A professional training program developed in 2005 by Kat Albrecht, a leading pioneer of the lost pet industry.

**MuzzleUp! Project ™**: An advocacy organization founded in 2013 whose purpose is to educate the public about dog behavior, safety, and why dogs who are muzzled don't need to be feared.

**Nose target**: Dog touches an object or designated spot with the nose.

**Olfactory**: The sensory system used for smelling.

**Operant-conditioning**: A learning method that employs rewards and punishments for behavior. Through Operant-conditioning, an association is made between a behavior and a consequence (whether negative or positive) for that behavior.

**Opposition Reflex**: The tendency for an organism to oppose physical pressure.

**Paw target**: Dog touches a designated object or spot with the paw.

**Periaqueductal Grey**: An area of grey matter in the mid-brain best known for its role in the inhibition of pain.

**Personality**: the unique set of characteristics, traits, and patterns of thinking, feeling, and behaving that distinguishes one individual dog from another.

**Poison**: To make a positive experience, treat or toy, etc., negative by associating it with something aversive.

**Salient**: Anything (person, behavior, trait, etc.) that is prominent, conspicuous, or otherwise noticeable compared with its surroundings.

**Self-Awareness**: The ability of organisms to recognize that they are separate from other organisms, while also assessing their own thoughts, feelings, and beliefs.

**Sentient**: The ability to perceive or respond to sensations of whatever kind—sight, hearing, touch, taste, or smell.

**Shaping**: A behavioral modification/training technique that involves reinforcing behaviors that get closer and closer to a desired target behavior.

> **Free Shaping**: Reinforcing a variety of behaviors to develop a shaping behavior repertoire, without a specific target behavior in mind.
>
> **Lure Shaping**: Using a lure or prompt to encourage behaviors that get closer and closer to the desired target behavior, and reinforcing those behaviors along the way.
>
> **Pure Shaping**: Reinforcing behaviors that get closer and closer to a desired target behavior without doing any luring or prompting.

**Sniffari**: Opportunity for a dog (or other organism) to freely explore the environment without interference from an accompanying human.

**SniffSpot™**: A company that contracts with landowners to rent their properties on an hourly basis to dogs and their humans as private dog parks—https://www.sniffspot.com/

**Specific Scent Discrimination**: A trained skill in which dogs (and some other animals) identify and isolate a particular target scent, such as a person or animal's unique odor. This skill is vital in roles like search and rescue and missing pet detection, where dogs must ignore irrelevant scents to find a specific person, animal or object.

**Splitting**: The recommended approach to Shaping; breaking the goal behavior down into very small steps and reinforcing very gradually to the final behavior.

**Subjectivity**: The ability to understand that other organisms have their own perspectives and beliefs, which can be communicated and influenced by their context and interactions with others.

**Theory of Mind**: The ability to understand and attribute mental states like beliefs, desires, intentions, and emotions to oneself and others.

**Threshold**: The level at which a trigger stimulus (a dog, child, situation, etc.) is presented at a strong enough intensity that the dog notices it, but is just below the level of intensity that would cause a strong emotional reaction.

**Volition**: The cognitive process by which an individual decides on and commits to a particular course of action.

# About the Author

Pat Miller is the author of many best-selling books on dog training and behavior, including *The Power of Positive Dog Training, Beware of the Dog, Positive Perspectives, Positive Perspectives 2, Play with Your Dog,* and *How to Foster Dogs.* Pat is the co-compiler/editor of *Veterinary Cooperative Care.* She published more than 500 articles in *The Whole Dog Journal* and served as training editor for the WDJ for 25 years.

Pat has worked professionally with animals her entire life. She worked at the Marin Humane Society in Novato, California from 1976 to 1996, first as a volunteer, then as Field Supervisor. She was the Director of Operations for ten years. During this time, she obtained an Associate Degree in Administration of Justice and a BS in Business Administration.

Pat moved to California's Central Coast in 1996, where her husband Paul was Director of Operations at Monterey SPCA. There she launched Peaceable Paws and served on the Board of the Santa Cruz SPCA. She was elected to the Board of Association of Professional Dog Trainers and is past President of that organization. She is a past Board member of the Certification Council for Professional Dog Trainers (CCPDT) and current Board member of the Animal Positive Coalition.

Pat and Paul moved to Fairplay, Maryland in 2004 where they live on their 80-acre farm with three dogs, four cats, two horses, and a pot-bellied pig. There they operate their force-free dog training and horse boarding facility. Pat is currently Director of the Peaceable Paws Trainer Academies and Training Programs.

In May of 2015, Pat was named by *Dog Fancy Magazine* as one of 45 people who have changed the dog world. In October of 2018, she was given a Lifetime Achievement Award by the Association of Professional Dog Trainers in recognition of her numerous and significant contributions to the dog training and behavior profession. In 2024, two of her books, *The Power of Positive Dog Training* and *Do-Over Dogs*, were included on the U.S. News' list of 8 best dog books. Pat can be reached at pat@peaceablepaws.com.

# Index

# *Did you enjoy this book?*

## WRITE A REVIEW!

REVIEWS HELP OTHER READERS DECIDE ON THEIR NEXT BOOK! GO TO WWW.DOGWISE.COM AND SELECT A STAR RATING (1-5) THEN LEAVE SOME COMMENTS DESCRIBING WHAT YOU ENJOYED OR SOMETHING YOU LEARNED WHILE READING THIS BOOK!

Write a Review ×

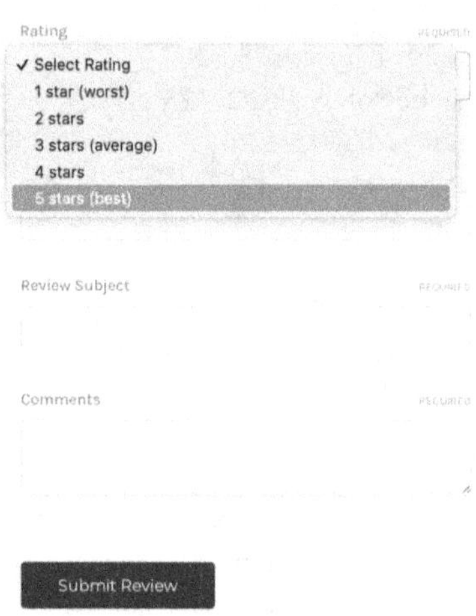

# Connect with us

FOLLOW, LIKE, AND TAG US ON SOCIAL MEDIA TO STAY CONNECTED

SCAN THE QR CODES BELOW WITH YOUR PHONE'S CAMERA APP TO GO DIRECTLY TO OUR SOCIAL MEDIA PROFILES

instagram
@dogwise.books

facebook
/dogwise

twitter
@DogwiseBooks